ABORTION
UNDER
ATTACK

WOMEN ON THE CHALLENGES FACING CHOICE

EDITED BY KRISTA JACOB

FOREWORD BY REBECCA WALKER/AFTERWORD BY GLORIA FELDT

SEAL PRESS

Abortion Under Attack
Women on the Challenges Facing Choice

Published by
Seal Press
An Imprint of Avalon Publishing Group, Incorporated
1400 65th Street, Suite 250
Emeryville, CA 94608

9 8 7 6 5 4 3 2 1
Library of Congress Cataloging-in-Publication Data

Jacob, Krista.
Abortion under attack : women on the challenges facing choice / Krista Jacob.
p. cm.
ISBN-13: 978-1-58005-185-9
ISBN-10: 1-58005-185-5
1. Abortion—United States. 2. Abortion—Moral and ethical aspects. 3. Pro-choice movement—United States. I. Title.

HQ767.5.U5A2827 2006
363.460973—dc22

2006021113

Interior design by Amber Pirker
Printed in the United States of America by Malloy
Distributed by Publishers Group West

For Jim, Maxwell & Colin, as always
And for Tamra, with love

CONTENTS

sick
baby

FOREWORD

REBECCA WALKER

THE ESSAYISTS IN THIS ANTHOLOGY TACKLE THE THORNY ISSUES that any human being who cares about women and children, men and the family, wants to see addressed within the abortion debate.

We are encouraged to allow for the emotional complexity of the abortion experience, and instructed on the multiple uses of RU-486. We are asked if there even is such an isolated event as an abortion, and if so, what do we call reductive selection, or the removal of an ectopic pregnancy?

We hear from a young woman who sometimes wishes she were aborted, and from a pro-choice Catholic leader who dares to ask the most relevant question of all: Can't we uphold the right to terminate pregnancy and acknowledge the sanctity of human life at the same time?

We are reminded that the concept of "reproductive choice" is restricted to a privileged few, whereas the need for "reproductive justice" is pervasive. We are given new "frames" à la George Lakoff. Instead of calling ourselves "pro-choice," one writer offers, we should assert ourselves to be "pro-rights," something no Constitution-thumping American can possibly deny.

At this critical point in the struggle to secure the most basic reproductive rights for all women, this book is a weapon, a tool, a necessary resource. The power of this volume is in the variety of its voices, the multiplicity of its approach. Krista Jacob's insistence on a nuanced exploration that allows for plenty of gray is paramount to the significance of this work.

For the last fifteen years, I have presented three simple points to individuals and organizations loosely identified as "the women's movement":

1. The movement must be presented in a way that attempts to connect to the current zeitgeist, not unlike an ad campaign. Movement aesthetic must be organic to its time, and forged with the intent of a seduction so powerful, its ideas spread like a virus. Silence = Death. "I'm Black and I'm Proud." "M&M's melt in your mouth, not in your hands."

Sometimes this language explodes organically from the populace, and sometimes it is crafted in focus groups. The only credible measure of its success is effectiveness. Are our constituents getting more of their needs met? If not, our language isn't working and needs to be retooled.

2. The movement cannot shy away from complexity and contradiction. To the contrary, it should be informed by the constantly changing nature of all things, and incorporate this

fundamental truth into its ideology and strategies. This fluidity gives the movement the ultimate tool: the ability to change position, to morph, without being in contradiction to itself. Freedom from status quo thinking within political communities creates the possibility for constant innovation.

3. The strategy and execution of the movement must be elevated to the level of genius. Harriet Tubman was not an ordinary woman, but a visionary tactician. Her work was the result of intellect, intuition, passion, faith, and, we can assume, a very high standard of engagement with the issues at hand. Harriet Tubman was not content to be an ordinary freedom fighter. She wanted to be a master freedom fighter. A revolutionary genius.

Our movement needs research and development. Well-funded think tanks. Intergenerational camaraderie. The best minds, female *and* male. Artists. Physicists. Venture capitalists. Engineers. Bio-geneticists. Our movement needs fearlessness. Originality. Openness.

In other words: "Mediocrity Equals Death."

Abortion Under Attack succeeds because it fulfills these three requirements and more. Until we learn to talk about abortion in a way that resonates with the contemporary moment, until we create strategy that is blinding in its brilliance, until we embrace complexity so completely that it becomes our ally rather than our undoing, we will be perpetually behind opponents who set both the timing and the tenor of the debate.

Read this book and be inspired, encouraged, and most of all, introduced to the future.

Rebecca Walker *is a best-selling author, an acclaimed speaker and teacher, and an award-winning visionary and activist in the fields of intergenerational feminism, enlightened masculinity, and transformational human awareness. When she was just twenty-five,* Time *magazine named her one of the fifty most influential future leaders of America—an award which has since been followed by many others, including the Women Who Could Be President Award from the League of Women Voters, the Champion of Choice Award from California Abortion and Reproductive Rights Action League, and the Women of Distinction Award from the American Association of University Women. In 1995, Walker published* To Be Real: Telling the Truth and Changing the Face of Feminism, *which has been in print for more than ten years. In 2002, Rebecca's memoir,* Black, White, and Jewish: Autobiography of a Shifting Self, *became an international bestseller and won the Alex Award from the American Library Association. She published* What Makes a Man: Twenty-Two Writers Imagine the Future *in 2004, and her next book,* Baby Love, *will be published in 2007.*

INTRODUCTION

KRISTA JACOB

ABORTION UNDER ATTACK IS A COLLECTION OF WOMEN'S STORIES
and feelings about abortion. From brave and controversial to sincere
and poignant, they reflect diverse perspectives on abortion and they represent the range and depth of what it means to be an advocate for reproductive rights.

Second-wave feminists taught us that personal experiences can be
political issues. And it is precisely because abortion is both a personal
experience and a political issue that the essays contained in these pages
are so rich and compelling. Some of the writers focus on the politics surrounding abortion; others share their personal stories; still others highlight their work to support those who have experienced abortion. These
writings embrace the complexities of a profoundly personal experience
within our culture—and a particular time in our history—that deeply

politicize abortion. *Abortion Under Attack* features what both sides have left out of the debate: the vast spectrum of experiences with, and opinions about, abortion within the reproductive rights movement.

Each of these writers shares a commitment to education about abortion and to making society a better, safer, and more just place for all people—families and individuals alike. Laura Fraser writes about the dangers of a government that restricts mifepristone, a drug that's used to terminate early pregnancies, but that has also proven effective in treating fibroids, endometriosis, and depression. Frances Kissling, President of Catholics for a Free Choice, argues that we can engage in meaningful conversations about the potential value of fetal life (rather than leaving it in the hands of pro-life leaders) and still hold firm the belief that the legal rights of the woman take precedence. Elizabeth Wardle, a former pro-life activist, deconstructs the rhetoric of abortion and draws connections between abortion and other social issues, such as the minimum wage, universal healthcare, sexuality education, and adoption laws. Patricia Justine Tumang provides an eloquent account of her abortion and subsequent self-recovery. Amy Richards challenges the pro-choice movement to adopt language that strips conservatives of their moral authority as defenders of "life." Diana Huet de Guerville shares her painful story of being unwanted by her father and how that led to her work to protect legal abortion.

Asian Communities for Reproductive Justice (ACRJ), an organization at the forefront of the reproductive rights movement, provides a well-researched historical account of reproductive issues. ACRJ has created an important theoretical paradigm in which abortion is contextualized within a woman's lived experience and placed within a much larger social justice framework. Their work is helping to expand the dialogue on reproductive rights so that more voices, not just those primarily concerned about abortion rights, can be brought into the discussion. Their work is strengthening our movement and reminds us that alliances must be built among unlikely allies.

Abortion Under Attack brings different, often contradictory, always illu-minating, views together under one larger unified philosophy, albeit one that some writers give different labels: pro-choice, pro-rights, pro-voice, and pro-reproductive justice. I hope that *Abortion Under Attack* will serve as a call to action for those who are conflicted or resolved about their stance on abortion, and for new and veteran pro-choice activists alike.

THE NEW LANGUAGE OF ABORTION

In fall 2005, the political climate was reaching an apex that was mak-ing me and other activists and writers nervous. The collision of Supreme Court justice vacancies, pharmacists' refusal to fill prescriptions for the Pill, legislation banning late-term abortions, and more, presented them-selves in such rapid-fire succession that it seemed time to act. Over the course of the many months that I've been working on this anthology, *Roe v. Wade* has become further jeopardized; abortion access is rapidly erod-ing at the state level. (As I write this Introduction, the South Dakota state legislature has voted to outlaw all abortions—even when rape or incest is involved—except to save the life of the mother.) Other personal fac-tors came together for me as well, allowing a book like this to be a reality where previously it could not have happened. My two young sons started preschool, I was in the middle of a career change, and, after a two-year-long hiatus (ironically because I was overwhelmed by the responsibilities of early motherhood), I had begun to reengage in abortion politics.

It was clear that it was time to engage in a new conversation and to explore some of the new ideas that had emerged—such as making room for exploring the notion of fetal pain and women's grief after an abor-tion experience—even though these ideas challenge the platform the pro-choice movement has fought so hard to develop and maintain. But I was interested in the new ways that some pro-choice people are think-ing and talking about abortion. By speaking out, they are creating a new abortion dialogue that is firmly rooted in support of legal abortion, yet they seek to unravel the layers of "grayness" that comprise the abortion issue. I have witnessed the way this dialogue has translated into political action. It is part of a nascent grassroots movement coalescing within the larger pro-choice movement—it's a movement within a movement—and like so many grassroots movements before, it's being built from the ground up. This movement has been shaped by the abortion stories of those who work in the clinics and promoted by those who are less visible within the more mainstream reproductive rights movement, such as pro-choice people of color, liberal religious activists, and abortion providers. These are the voices I sought to include in this anthology, along with women who have long been a part of the mainstream movement, but who are open enough to recognize that there's a sea change afoot—one that is not only out of their hands, but also doesn't have to challenge their core values about women's right to choose.

Over the course of three months, I received over one hundred submissions for this anthology. It was clear, as I read the essays, that changes that had seemed more like whispers in the wind were in fact becoming a small grassroots movement that has taken hold. The dialogue is evolving and quietly influencing the discourse on abortion. It is paving the way for the middle-of-the-roaders to actively join our movement.

But as I moved forward, I was poignantly aware of my own reluctance to embrace some of these changes. This new dialogue on abortion has set off a buzz of controversy among some in the larger pro-choice movement. It tackles issues of religion, spirituality, and the morality of abortion; it includes the voices of those who are pro-choice but who also have significant moral and/or personal conflicts with abortion; it includes women's stories of grief, sadness, and remorse about their abortion experience; it fosters conversations about the nature of "life" and the potential humanness of the fetus; and it even recognizes that a person can view a zygote, an embryo, or a fetus as a life (and that abortion kills that life) and still hold strong the belief that abortion must remain a safe, legal, and dignified experience accessible to any woman who needs it. This new dialogue allows for a person's feelings about abortion to change over the course of their life, and that at one point a "choice" can feel simple and easy, and at another point it can feel profoundly tragic and morally charged. This dialogue embraces ethnically and racially diverse voices and recognizes that the concept of "choice" is flawed when placed in the context of poverty, race, culture, and oppression.

This new dialogue also includes the paradox of abortion and control: while abortion can be an act of empowerment—the act of asserting control over one's body and taking action to determine the course of one's future—it is also true that the need to have an abortion can be the result of a *lack of control* over one's life, personally, financially, or otherwise. The Alan Guttmacher Institute concluded that 58–67 percent of women who were sexually or physically abused or exposed to frequent psychological distress as children have unintended first pregnancies (compared to 37–41 percent of their peers who did not experience this kind of abuse). We also know now that sexual abuse can increase risky behavior among teens and subsequently contribute to unintended pregnancy. In short, a lack of control can lead a woman or girl to need an abortion. Choice, then, gives her back some degree of control.

But, as with most political discourse, this new dialogue itself exists on a continuum, and includes viewpoints of those who are not conflicted about the nature or morality of abortion. Equally important to this conversation are women who have no religious or spiritual reservations about abortion and who did not experience any negative feelings after their abortion. Many of these individuals still possess an integrated awareness of (and respect for) those with moral qualms about abortion. Well-known feminist activist Jennifer Baumgardner, a contributor to this anthology, started the I'm Not Sorry campaign *(www.imnotsorry.net)* which honors and empowers women who don't feel sad or ashamed about their abortion and affirms for women that they are not bad or selfish people for having had an abortion. Baumgardner's campaign is important because it enriches this new dialogue by honoring the unconflicted and unapologetic, and it validates the women who need the reinforcement that they are not "baby killers" or "immoral" or "evil" or any of the other cruel judgments leveled against them.

It's always difficult to highlight controversies within controversial subjects, which is why I was somewhat hesitant about putting together a book that showcases the discontinuities and discontents within our movement. Abortion is under serious attack, on all fronts, and I am well aware of the potential consequences of airing our dirty laundry (or suggesting that our movement needs to open up to more perspectives on abortion and make changes in how we talk about it). I am not calling into question the hard work that the women and men of our movement have done to provide my generation with the freedoms and opportunities we wouldn't otherwise have had. I present this anthology with the awareness that, because this dialogue honors the "grayness" of the abortion issue, it might sometimes be taken out of context and milked for its shock value. In fact, this new dialogue has already been manipulated to serve the political agendas of those who oppose legal abortion. Truly understanding the layers of this dialogue requires the ability to think critically, feel empathy and compassion for those whose experiences are very different from our own, and to think beyond political slogans and agendas. This is a tall order in a culture that is developing a shortage of both critical thinking and compassion.

But, as my friend Peg Johnston says, "The truth is more solid ground to stand on," and she's right. We can't paint all abortion experiences in one stroke. Women are unique individuals, and so are their experiences with and feelings about abortion. As *Abortion Under Attack* illustrates, we don't all have to adhere to a "right" standard of how to think or feel about abortion, and we certainly cannot use a single yardstick to measure the extent of what abortion means to women and men. We need only to be honest about our lives and our experiences.

MY PERSONAL EVOLUTION

I was first introduced to this new dialogue in 1997 when I began working as a reproductive health counselor at a women's clinic that provided abortions. Truth be told, I didn't buy it. It smacked of pro-life propaganda. After all, I grew up with legal abortion and had heard the terrible stories of illegal abortion and the laments of those forced to have children before they were ready to be pregnant or to be a parent. Though I've always understood that abortion may not be an easy issue for some people, it seemed to me a relatively straightforward issue: A woman needs to have the right to control her reproduction. Period.

However, my experiences as an abortion counselor proved very different, and taught me that there should be a comma where I had put a period.

As a counselor, I saw shocking contradictions. I heard some patients use the words "killing" and "baby" in the same sentence when talking about their abortion. Our clinic had a "hostile consent" form that we asked pro-life patients to sign before their abortion which stated that though they were technically opposed to abortion, they were still giving their full consent to have one. The first time I witnessed a patient rejoin the pro-life protesters in front of our clinic after her abortion, I was so angry I almost broke patient confidentiality (amidst the rosaries and posters depicting chopped-up fetuses). One of my patients had been driven to the clinic by her priest, who later performed a "mock baptism" and prayed with the patient afterward for forgiveness. This woman was certain that she wanted an abortion, but she was also a Catholic who desperately craved the support and help of her priest. He was willing to support her. I also discovered that many women's options were so limited that they didn't view their decision to have an abortion as much of a "choice." As one patient who became pregnant while being prostituted told me, "'My body, my choice' doesn't apply to me." My political activism in college brought me to the abortion issue, yet most of my patients had no political or historical awareness about abortion (nor did they realize that pre–1973 we all could have gone to jail for our collective roles in helping to terminate their pregnancy).

Admittedly, I struggled with my own philosophical growing pains, but eventually I opened up and began to learn from my patients' stories. I saw a significant disconnect between the politics of the issue and the actual women and men choosing abortion. This work defied all of my stereotypes about what abortion means in the life of people who experience it, and it demanded that I set aside my simplified political understanding of it. While it's true that the right to control reproduction is inextricably linked to women's rights politically, economically, socially, and so on, it is also true that there is a deeper, more personal aspect of abortion where the politics of the issue play a limited role.

Legal abortion has saved women's lives and benefited millions of women and men in a myriad of ways. Though the obstacles today come in the form of abortion restrictions (which make it very difficult and sometimes impossible to get access to an abortion), the actual expense of the abortion, and in the shame, silence, and stigma that surrounds this issue, legal abortion has, in general, allowed women and men to experience abortion more fully without the fear of going to jail, or being butchered, or causing themselves serious physical harm by taking medical matters into their own hands. When people have this freedom, they have space to think more deeply about what abortion means to them, how they truly feel about terminating a pregnancy, how their loved ones feel about it, and how their decision may affect their friends and family and any other aspect of their lives.

The fact that some pro-choice people are talking about abortion in new ways reflects a natural and healthy progression of a social movement that needs to be responsive to a changing and evolving society. It isn't "selling out" or "giving in" or even making a compromise. It simply demonstrates that we are listening to women's words, and that our political movement is growing to reflect the collective stories of the millions of people who have experienced abortion. The inclusion of these theoretical frameworks is a tribute to the successes of our movement, not a betrayal of it. To be sure, it is as much our right to have different feelings about abortion as it is our right to have access to a safe abortion.

Krista Jacob
March 2006

WHAT IS ABORTION?

AMY RICHARDS

IN THE SPRING OF 2005, GEORGE LAKOFF, THE INSIGHTFUL, practical, and smart linguist, challenged abortion proponents to reconsider their use of "choice" rhetoric. Responding to the backpedaling by otherwise progressive individuals (chair of the Democratic National Committee Howard Dean and Senator Hillary Rodham Clinton, to name two), Lakoff was attempting to rescue this debate from right-wing zealots, who, in his determination, are actually "creating unwanted pregnancies." In his article, "The Foreign Language of Choice," published by the online journal *AlterNet*, Lakoff pushed for the adoption of more proactive language that focused on an individual's personal freedom and moved away from the linguistically inaccurate word "choice." He argued that the concept of "choice" is less serious and derives from a consumer, rather than a moral, vocabulary.

Many in the pro-choice community responded angrily, blaming Lakoff for contributing to conservative interpretations of the abortion issue. The same accusations were unleashed against Hillary Clinton when she referred to abortion as a "sad, even tragic choice"; Dean, who emphasized that abortion is a decision of personal freedom, thus de-emphasizing it as a woman's issue and not vehemently endorsing it as a right; John Kerry, who confessed in his presidential bid that he believes life begins at conception; and even the paramount pro-choice group NARAL Pro-Choice America, which penned "An Open Letter to the Right-to-Life Community," in which it called for a joint commitment to reduce the number of abortions. The proposal to reframe the language in these instances—as well as numerous others—was only heard as negative; it was perceived as fodder for the Right or a capitulation that "they" have the moral high ground. Yet, these perspectives come directly from organizations that have been leaders in this struggle and from individuals who maintain that they unconditionally support a woman's basic access to abortion, though with varying degrees of restrictions, such as waiting periods and parental consent laws.

In my assessment, these leaders were simply amplifying what they hear from the majority of their constituents—those who support access to testing and procedures that thoughtfully help women determine whether or not to continue a pregnancy, who are sympathetic allies and patients alike but don't want to be associated with the politically divisive movements for abortion rights and choice. In other words, it's not the reality of abortion that's at stake; it's the rhetoric. In traversing this country, speaking to thousands of college students, and interacting with random, unsolicited, unconverted individuals through my online advice column "Ask Amy," which has existed at *www.feminist.com* since 1995, I see reflections of this discourse and reasons for what is synopsized as a declining number of pro-choice allies. (According to the semifamous annual study conducted on UCLA's incoming freshman class, the support for abortion rights has been on a steady decline since the early 1990s. Today it hovers at barely over 50 percent.)

Though fewer people affiliate themselves with the labels "pro-choice" and "abortion rights advocate," the real question is: What does the general public think these terms represent? Support might be waning for this impersonal political terminology, but people—through their actions and expressions—support the actual procedures that underscore the complexity that surrounds the abortion debate. If we were to measure "support for abortion rights" by those who access this right in contrast to how people answer public opinion polls, which don't leave much gray area for the nuances of such a complicated issue, there would be no debate about what the majority opinion was. Abortion providers are resistant to put this "political" pressure on their patients because they think it infringes on their privacy or personal freedoms. However, the reasons that most people must turn to abortion providers in the first place are political—cuts in federal funding for food, housing, and other subsidies make it impossible for some to consider having a child; already high and rising health care costs make mainstream health care prohibitive; and abstinence-only education, which is mandated by any school receiving federal dollars, misinform people about their options and also shun, indirectly, those who might have made a mistake and had sex out of wedlock. Beyond abortion itself, there are a plethora of issues covered under this umbrella—birth control, HIV/AIDS testing, prenatal care, etc.—services that are often only available through Planned Parenthood affiliates and otherwise progressively inclined clinics across the country. Point being, the politics are driving people to these places and decisions in the first place, and in my assessment, we owe it to the masses (and to our belief in our own movement) to translate that.

The current looming threat (or hope, depending on your perspective), and thus ensuing dialogue, is that *Roe v. Wade*, the 1973 Supreme Court decision which technically legalized abortion in the United States, will be overturned. With two recent Bush-appointed Supreme Court justices, the rally cry from abortion rights proponents has been "Save *Roe*," presuming that the current court would overturn it. (Of course, that would require a case that would challenge it in the first place.) Though *Roe* codified access to abortion in all fifty states, the current debate brings to light an even more pressing and tangible question: For whom is abortion even legal? The women who would be penalized if *Roe* were to be overturned are already facing extreme limitations: money—a first-trimester abortion costs in the range of $400 to $600; access—providers are clustered in urban areas, leaving rural women with limited resources or heinous drives; waiting periods; parental consent laws; and confusion—for instance, not wanting the child, but feeling pressured by others to go through with the pregnancy. These are just a handful of complications that make it practically illegal, even with *Roe,* for a majority of women who want an abortion to obtain one. This begs the question: Whose rights does *Roe v. Wade* protect if white, middle-class, urban women will continue to have access to abortion even in the absence of *Roe?* These are the women who will have the resources to fly to states or countries where the procedure isn't criminalized, or to visit their family doctor, who will creatively call the procedure by another name.

We've all heard stories about an anti-choice protestor having to cross her own picket line to get an abortion, or the Catholic woman who swore, out of religious loyalty, that she would never have an abortion—that is until a severe fetal abnormality was detected and an abortion was suddenly a "medical necessity." I remember the story of one woman who was interviewed a few years ago in *The New York Times* for an article on prenatal testing about her decision to have a second-trimester abortion after the fetus was diagnosed with a fetal abnormality. When the reporter questioned her about her abortion, the woman clarified, "I don't look at it as though I had an abortion, even though that is technically what it is. . . . There's a difference. I wanted this baby." Another woman told me that her selective reduction, a procedure used to terminate one or more fetuses in cases of multiple pregnancies that is increasingly common with the use of infertility drugs and other assisted reproductive technologies (as well as "advanced maternal age"), wasn't an abortion, it was ordered by the doctor. And a friend who had an ectopic pregnancy that was terminated, as the majority of these pregnancies are due to the risk to the mother and the fetus, claims she didn't have an abortion— though her pregnancy was unexpected, she says she would have had a D&X (dilation and extraction), the most common procedure used during first-trimester terminations, if greater medical care hadn't been required. As annoying as it is to hear women qualify their experiences and distance themselves from a mythical "other woman," in some ways they aren't so far off. There isn't an actual procedure called abortion—abortion is the conclusion, but the process is more nuanced.

Besides evolving terminology, a larger issue to consider is that perhaps we have outgrown *Roe*. *Roe* was argued on the grounds of privacy, and the justices adamantly stated that they weren't medical experts and thus were not equipped to answer certain questions in the debate, including when life begins. "We need not resolve the difficult question of when life begins," Supreme Court Justice Blackmun wrote in his majority opinion. "When those trained in the respective disciplines of medicine, philosophy, and theology are unable to arrive at any consensus, the judiciary, at this point in the development of man's knowledge, is not in a position to speculate as to the answer." Today, this most talked-about decision tends to play out as being solely about procedures that terminate pregnancies—resulting in less privacy on this issue than in the pre-*Roe* days. "[A] woman enjoyed a substantially broader right to terminate a pregnancy than she does in most States today," stated the decision. The law itself was written before the onslaught of assisted reproductive technologies and significant advancements in scientific and medical data, which can now tease out much more information about the fetus. Semantics around viability and what it means to save the "life and health" of the mother are constantly debated and in flux. Given the fact that natural changes in the debate are inevitable, reconsidering *Roe* doesn't necessarily mean the end of access to abortion.

Abortion became "legal" with *Roe v. Wade,* but it existed in this country for hundreds of years prior, and with far less debate. Based on British Common Law, the general consensus was that abortion was permissible until "quickening"—the first movements of the fetus, usually around sixteen to eighteen weeks, well into the second trimester. It wasn't until the mid to late 1800s that states began to enforce greater restrictions, or to codify abortion into law. The grounds for making abortion illegal had to do with concern about sexual promiscuity, the danger it presented to women, and protecting prenatal life—though those early laws clearly stated that protecting the mother's life was more important than protecting the fetus's. In the absence of effective anesthetics, the procedure itself was considered dangerous to women and thus legalizing it would have been interpreted as an endorsement of a hazardous procedure. In seeking ways to preserve the future of abortion rights in this country, this history is instructive.

Today, what people seem to react to is the word "abortion," a word that has multiple meanings and interpretations, but that is also wholly synonymous with a political debate about whether or not women should have access to procedures that allow them to terminate a pregnancy, wanted or unwanted. Politically, abortion is used as a litmus test and colloquially, to evaluate a person. People detect that others are judging them based solely on this label and thus reject this narrow conclusion. They aren't rejecting the content, but the terminology. They don't want to be boxed in when, in fact, their feelings on the subject are likely to be much more complicated and nuanced. Everyone has their own threshold: "What if she was raped?" "What if the fetus wouldn't survive anyway?" "What if it was her seventh child?" "What if it were me?" The same is true when it comes to restrictions: "She could have afforded to have a child." "She could have found a way to make it work." "What about all of the infertile couples?" But the truth is that the choice is so personal and the circumstances so unique that no one really knows what a given woman would do—and so it's pointless to speculate. While people are entitled to judge other people's decisions, they can simultaneously and quietly not stand in the way of access—and this is what the majority appear to lean toward.

With the seemingly stark delineations being drawn, those of us who freely embrace pro-choice rhetoric should pause and ask ourselves: "Is abortion an actual medical term or is it a political distinction? Or in my assessment, is it neither?" The procedures encompassed by this vague term actually range from medication to surgery, including: RU-486, a medication used to terminate an early pregnancy; D&X, the procedure most synonymous with late-term abortions (and the highly controversial so-called partial-birth abortion); selective reduction; or even delivery. The word "abortion" is inaccurate and doesn't begin to address the specificity of varying procedures. The Partial-Birth Abortion Ban Act brought this to light. The government essentially outlawed a procedure that didn't exist; it also overrode, for the first time, a counter-recommendation from the American Medical Association—thus confirming that the debate had been taken out of the hands of the medical establishment and was instead firmly rooted in political bureaucracy. To the extent that these procedures result in the termination of a pregnancy, "abortion" is appropriate, but then the label should also apply to miscarriages (you don't hear people debating the politics of those usually sad circumstances), emergency contraception (which may or may not be interrupting a pregnancy), and even stillborns.

Since there is no official procedure that is abortion, what does it really mean to say that one is a supporter of abortion rights? The political Right uses it as shorthand for the murder of unborn babies and, symbolically, to condemn people who support women's access to these choices, including, of course, anyone who has actually had an abortion. These women are assumed to be selfish, ignorant baby killers (saying nothing about the men involved in these choices, who are freed from this ridicule, even though they are almost assuredly stakeholders in the decision to end the pregnancy and equal participants in conception). The political Left uses abortion as a symbol of equality and emancipation, and also a single issue to galvanize around. These professional advocates (not necessarily the masses) tend to push abortion as symbolic of other issues, such as access to sex education, access to quality health care, etc. Historically, feminists called for abortion on demand without apology; today the debate seems to have neutralized to "it's a decision between a woman and her physician." During the 2004 presidential election, the Republicans made it shorthand for irresponsible, selfish women who either want to live off the state or for the women in the more privileged sect who want to have their cake and eat it, too; the Democrats used it to placate women, but only those select few who either need to be saved or who are twelve years old and desperate. The poster child for abortion access is usually someone in a dire situation, which is a debatable tactic. We ought not be in the business of determining whose choices, motivations, and circumstances to sanction.

As much as the pro-choice community has attempted to reframe the issue in terms of "choice" and "privacy" and "women's control of their bodies," the popular assumption is that supporting any one of these interpretations comes down to being pro-abortion. On the other side of the debate, "life" has been the favored term, used in an attempt to claim the moral high ground. This terminology also solidifies one's conviction that life begins at conception and that the person who holds this view is thus opposed to any interruption in this natural progression (putting aside for a moment the hypocrisy of those who hold this view and simultaneously support the death penalty, not to mention the common inconsistency that allows for exception when the life and health of the mother are at risk). Conservatives take their position so far that they have rallied to ban stem-cell research on the grounds that those cells are potential life, and even oppose contraception because "the human embryonic person dies." This all leads directly toward their larger goal of extending more rights to the fetus than to the woman. Regardless of the words used, the debate essentially comes around to whether or not one supports actual procedures that end a pregnancy and whether one trusts women to make this decision for themselves.

In lieu of finding common political ground, we have to prioritize rescuing this basic human right from the contested language. We have to think beyond the divisive rhetoric and give more attention to what we are really debating. The danger in perpetuating this narrow banter lies in its inaccuracy. Plus, with support allegedly dwindling, we have to find explanations beyond indirectly conceding that our country is moving in a more conservative direction; with barely 50 percent of eligible voters going to the polls, that seems like an implausible conclusion. When possible, we must use more accurate language. We cannot be so quick to judge others solely by how they answer one question. We have to take risks and be more honest about our own limitations while still being forthright about our conviction that access should still be legal and protected. It's possible for us to be personally conflicted without being politically compromised. And, while we strive to eliminate any negativity associated with abortion and choice, we can't do so at the expense of alienating our potential allies. Language is fluid—we should be deliberate and specific when it comes to word choice, and simultaneously resist any outside attempts to manipulate our stance. Rigid language doesn't serve the larger goal of preserving access to terminations and, more importantly, it doesn't serve women.

SEX, UNINTENDED PREGNANCY, AND POVERTY

One Woman's Evolution from "Choice" to "Reproductive Justice"

JENNY HIGGINS

As a nineteen-year-old feminist and college student, I temporarily left the privileged confines of my liberal-arts campus and began working as a medical assistant at an abortion clinic. "Choice" and "reproductive rights," which heretofore had seemed such unified and clarifying concepts, now appeared enormously stratified by class and race. This shift motivated a deeper personal and professional exploration of the connection between abortion and social injustice.

I WAS A FEMINIST BY THE TIME I WAS THIRTEEN. OR, MORE accurately, my feminist inklings presented themselves—reportedly—as early as my toddler years; but it wasn't until my early adolescence that I learned of the term and embraced it with fervor. At that time, I was thrilled by what feminism offered me; it gave voice and affirmation to sentiments I had long held but not named, and it presented the ground-work for an activist agenda that I could trust and support. Feminism provided not only a psychological haven of sorts, but also the inspiration to do more, be more, and to effect social change.

Like many young feminists in the United States, reproductive rights—and abortion rights in particular—were the first feminist principles I championed. I wore pro-choice buttons to school, slathered "U.S. OUT OF MY UTERUS" bumper stickers on my locker and notebooks, and argued passionately with peers and family members (or with just about anyone, really) about the salience of women's right to choose.

A few years later, as a new college student, I enrolled in women's studies classes and hungrily read up on reproductive rights, from both a historical and a theoretical perspective. I was one of many Western middle-class feminists who believed that if women had full autonomy over their sexuality, their bodies, and their reproductive desires and destinies, they could become truly socially liberated. An unabashed and unadulterated pro-choice stance was a requisite accompaniment to this belief.

Looking back on this younger version of myself, I'm envious of the clarity and simplicity offered by the feminist cocoon in which I first experienced transformation. When I innocently approached the issue on this pure and abstract level, abortion was always an acceptable option, no matter what the circumstances of the pregnancy. Abortion seemed to serve as a symbolic embodiment of women's autonomy, a harbinger of personal or social empowerment. That is, in exercising her right to choose, a woman was capitalizing on her personal freedom and power. As such, I associated abortion with positive, rights-based connotations, not with tinges of loss, poor decisions, or irresponsible behavior (e.g., not using contraception, even after numerous prior abortions), let alone larger social pathologies such as sexism, racism, or poverty.

Then I began working with real-life abortion patients. What a reckoning. The summer I turned nineteen, I called my local abortion clinic (at that time, one of two in the entire state) and asked if they had any job openings. While the clinic administrator hardly had summer jobs to offer in the technical sense of the term, she was—as is standard among clinics nationally—chronically short staffed due to rapid employee turnover. She had just lost a lab assistant, I would later learn, and was thrilled to have an immediate replacement. I went in for an interview, and by the end of the day, I was cleaning procedure rooms between patients, sterilizing surgical instruments, and packaging fetal material (what I learned to call "POC," which stood for "products of conception").

That day marked the beginning of my five-year stint in clinical abortion work. I would continue in a part-time capacity, both at the original clinic and at a subsequent one in the Southeast, where I moved for graduate school. Due to chronic understaffing, I moved from lab support to medical assistance to counseling, and also did everything in between. Our clients varied significantly in age, parity, and circumstance, but the clinic staff would counsel any woman who came to the door.

On some days, the clinics served as few as five women and on others, as many as one hundred. I spoke to women about their contraceptive options, held their hands, and helped them back into their clothes. I heard thousands of stories about sex, relationships, contraceptive use (or lack thereof), and the varying experience of being unhappily—often miserably—pregnant.

It was, at once, the most thrilling, transforming, and terrifying work I had ever done.

On one hand, I resided at the utter core of the movement. There is something uniquely grassroots, for example, about holding a woman's hand and telling her you support her decision, or wiping down an examining table after her abortion is complete. I was seduced by the notion that I was touching women's lives—as well as their bodies—in tangible ways that made their abortion experiences better. My work at the clinics took me to the very essence of women's reproductive experience, a responsibility I did not take lightly, but approached with empathy, care, and respect for dignity and choice.

On the other hand, my shifts were exhausting, confusing, and troubling. The underfunded structure of services at the clinics meant that I rarely had the time or resources to give women the clinical or psychological care they needed or deserved. Counseling sessions were strictly time constrained, sometimes allowing only five minutes per patient. I had to rush women out of the procedure room within minutes—sometimes seconds—of their terminations so that we could quickly prep the room for the next patient. This hustle meant another missed chance to provide follow-up counseling or assistance to help these women avoid future unintended pregnancies.

Also, I was disillusioned by the general dilapidation of the clinic: the dated medical equipment, the revolving door of staff, and other indications of a clinical setting with inadequate resources. Instead of serving as a reproductive rights midwife of sorts, helping women realize their own self-efficacy and autonomy, I felt like I was forced to provide rushed and inadequate care, which, by way of shoddy counseling, may have been contributing directly to women's poor contraceptive adherence in the future.

In a second challenge to my previously held beliefs, clinic work forced me to face the reality of abortion as real human calamity. It was hard to ignore abortion's underbelly of loss when so many patients exhibited deep and, at times, almost bottomless sadness, distress, or anxiety. Even though these women were trying to make the best decision for themselves, such certainty of choice couldn't entirely remove the psychological injury. While the reality of this loss didn't make me any less pro-choice, it did diminish the whole abortion-as-empowerment model I had held so dear. And it deepened my interest in the prevention side of reproductive health care. On numerous occasions, I found myself fantasizing about leaving abortion work and instead focusing on condom promotion or family planning. (Notably, today I research pregnancy and HIV prevention in an academic setting, with far more frequent contact with computers, books, and ideas than with patients.)

The third and most salient challenge was that abortion no longer seemed equally acceptable in all situations. A number of patients used—or abused, depending on one's moral perspective—their right to abortion in ways that forced me to question the depth of my own pro-choice stance. For example, I was deeply troubled by "repeaters," women who came to us for their third, fourth, or fifth abortion, and who often exhibited life-long histories of spotty—or no—contraceptive use. I also struggled with women who waited until well into their second trimester before present-ing themselves for elective terminations. These cases, which on the surface smacked of personal irresponsibility, vexed me because I felt they made the pro-choice platform even more vulnerable to critics. That is, a politi-cal safe haven for choice remained all the more elusive when abortion was requested late in the pregnancy and/or multiple times in a woman's life-time. I'm a bit hesitant to admit that the tough cases took a personal toll as well. They tarnished my innocently romanticized version of abortion as a difficult but worthy, and even admirable, decision. I was angry to feel alienated from the uncomplicated feminist principles which had been so essential and inspiring to me just years earlier.

Over time, I devised different strategies to address some of these challenges. For example, I would remind myself that late-term abortions, as well repeaters, make up only the tiniest percentages of the total number of termination patients in the United States each year. These few cases already dominate public debate and outcry about abortion; I didn't want to let these outliers determine my own intellectual and emo-tional response to the issue. In my humbler moments, I would also admit that regardless of my own moral imperative, I could only apply that im-perative on my own actions; other women's pregnancy decisions weren't mine to make. After all, I didn't want to be guilty of the very same moral hijacking that characterizes the anti-abortion movement. And perhaps the most important mechanism I developed was to step back from the individual to the structural, or from the micro to the macro, as it were. That is, I began to consider abortion as reflective not only of women's individual decisions, but also of larger societal constraints and social inequalities, especially along the lines of gender and social class.

Not surprisingly, gender inequality is perhaps the easiest way to spot abortion's structural patterns. Unintended pregnancy and abortion are highly gendered phenomena, for both physiologic and social reasons. That women, and not men, seek care at the clinics is not only due to the fact that women are the ones who get pregnant. Cultural norms saddle women with the responsibility for pregnancy prevention, as well as with the consequences of unintended pregnancies, whether they end in abortion *or* birth. Men have far less social motivation to actively avoid pregnancies through contraception or condoms. Further, with a social premium placed on men's sexual pleasure, some men may often try to convince—if not coerce—women into using no contraceptive method at all, particularly condoms. Some men may want a pregnancy even when their partners don't, and/or they may pressure a woman into bringing the pregnancy to full term, even if she doesn't want to—a request made far more easily by someone who will not have to provide emotional or financial support for the child unless he so chooses. (Several of the women who waited until their second trimester to seek terminations told stories along these lines, or they spoke of how their partners would say they wanted the child but would then skip town.) Gendered social inequality means that women are far more socially dependent than men on romantic relationships.

There are compelling structural reasons, then, why women might deliberately abandon contraceptive use or fail to demand that their partner wear a condom. Unprotected sex may have the benefit of enhancing intimate relationships with men, one of women's most important forms of social capital. Until sexism and gendered power imbalance are eradicated, it is difficult to imagine how all women could be utterly and freely enabled to use contraception effectively and/or to capitalize on their right to abortion in an empowered or sagacious manner.

Gender's structural effect on abortion connects intimately with the influence of other forms of social inequality. Due in particular to race, ethnicity, and social class, the tools necessary to avoid unintended pregnancy are not equally accessible to all women. For example, we almost never serviced wealthier women at the clinics where I worked. In the Southeastern clinic, which was in an urban area, the majority of the clients were African American.

Two major reasons explain the absence of privileged women. First, they are more likely to have access to higher quality, private abortion care, either due to their insurance plans or because they can afford to pay out-of-pocket for such services. Second, I would later learn, wealthier women have less need for abortion services in general due to more consistent contraception use. They experience fewer unintended pregnancies than poor women. With the exception of middle-class teenagers (who could not risk filing with their insurance agency and having their parents learn about the abortion) or middle-class women temporarily lacking health insurance, abortion patients are overwhelmingly low-income and uninsured.

The middle class and elite, it seems, are relatively protected from unintended pregnancy in two major ways. First, they are protected from "risky" sex by way of their more consistent disease-prevention practices. To be sure, the privileged are not inherently more intelligent or efficacious than the poor. Yet because of promising educational and professional opportunities, as well as the perceived costs of premature (i.e., teenage) childbearing in middle-class communities, they are far more motivated to avoid pregnancy in the first place. Unlike poor teenagers, most middle-class adolescents can reasonably expect to attend college, if not graduate school, and to find comparatively reward-ing employment. Because the meanings and consequences of pregnancy are so different in higher- versus lower-class communities, contraceptive use is, understandably, also different depending on class.

Second, and more centrally to my own abortion work, the privi-leged can avoid subpar health services that may perpetuate phenomena that can contribute to unintended pregnancies in the first place—in par-ticular, rushed contraceptive counseling and profiling that contributes to poor contraceptive use. Even though I prided myself on providing at-tentive and empathic care to the patients with whom I worked, the clinic infrastructure and patient overload prohibited the kind of service that members of the middle and upper classes have come to expect—or the kind of care I had received at relatively posh student health centers or private gynecologist offices.

Privacy, for example, was a rare luxury at the clinics, especially on high-traffic procedure days. On Saturdays, women waited in the hall-ways for hours in flimsy medical gowns, already counseled and medi-cated, but queued in a long line of patients waiting to see the doctor. Sometimes even counseling was done in groups to save time, ten or fif-teen women sitting in a circle, holding their consent forms as they lis-tened to me speak. At other times, I was strictly limited to a five-minute counseling session for each patient. This is hardly sufficient time to as-certain the woman's consent, inform her of what to expect during and after the procedure, and counsel about contraceptives so that she could better avoid future unintended pregnancies.

Yet, as most of us who have worked in the abortion field know all too well, both the clinics' clients and the staff have little choice. Patients have few options for alternative sources of care given the dearth of pub-lic abortion providers nationwide. We tried to accommodate as many women as we could, which often meant that "extras," such as exten-sive counseling or follow-up care, were out of the question. Within the context I've described, abortion seemed less like an undivided right and more like a practice whose delivery depended greatly on one's wealth, insurance status, and access to the social and cultural resources that help avert unintended pregnancy.[1] For poor women, then, especially those faced with their second, third, or fourth unintended pregnancies, abortion can be less a symbol of self-efficacy or "choice" and more an indication of social inequality, social limitations, and reproductive injustice.

I am thirty years old now, and still fully supportive of abortion rights. In many ways, I am even more of an advocate for family planning and abortion on demand than I was at the age of thirteen. And despite my stated struggles, my time at the clinics remains the most meaningful and satisfying work I have ever done. Even now, as a holder of a PhD and an MPH, and as a researcher of gender, sexuality, HIV, and reproductive health at an Ivy League university, there are still days when I wonder why I ever left the clinic. That said, as I've described here, my work in the abortion field also destabilized my simplistic feminist beliefs about reproductive rights. These days, I take a different approach.

Following the lead of some of our movement's wisest and fiercest shepherds (special thanks to Angela Davis, Loretta Ross, and others),[2] I have come to adopt a framework of *reproductive justice*. This model moves beyond the individual, or micro, and demands a keen awareness of social inequality at the structural, or macro, level. While women's entitlement to bodily autonomy and free and informed choice are still central to this approach, so too is protection from exploitation or iniquity based on class, race and ethnicity, sexual orientation, or nationality.

Reproductive justice requires that women from all implicated social and demographic groups are themselves able to devise and voice their own needs and agendas. All women shouldn't be forced to inherit, by default, the feminist platform established by white, middle-class, Western feminists, especially if its liberal feminist centralization of reproductive rights, equal wages, better childcare, and greater representation of women in the public sphere doesn't capture their most pressing social concerns. While reproductive freedom should be available to all, we must recognize that the priorities of privileged women are not parallel with those of most other women in the world. Research and collaborative activist efforts in a number of developing countries[3] indicate that, for many women in resource-poor settings across the world, the right to abortion is hardly the top item on a feminist social agenda. Although the right to reproductive autonomy is likely to be on the list, more pressing priorities can include clean water, cessation of war and violence, reduction of exploitation in the global workplace (i.e., fair wages for women and men), or reductions in government corruption. The concept of reproductive "choice" may have little resonance in these settings.

Similarly, among many of the poor clients who came to the clinics, greater "choice" in the form of better access to or knowledge of contraception or abortion did not emerge as a particularly salient need or goal. Women I spoke with then, and whom I have interviewed for my research more recently, talked more often about the challenges of poverty or public assistance (or lack thereof), neighborhood crime, alarming rates of incarceration of black men in their community, and lack of educational opportunities and meaningful employment. My hope is that through a reproductive justice approach, any feminist agenda will include these issues (e.g., poverty reduction, crackdowns on race profiling, and better schools), even as we continue to strive for sexual autonomy and improved reproductive health services and policies.

An example that helps further explain the rationale of reproductive justice can be seen in the 2004 March for Women's Lives, a ground-shaking feminist event in Washington, D.C., in which I and one million other women participated. In its planning stages, the event had been entitled the "March for Choice," a phrase reflective of the centrality of reproductive rights to mainstream, middle-class, U.S. feminism. Women of color from within the movement, aided by the Atlanta-based SisterSong Collective, were forced to remind middle-class, white organizers that the term "choice" has class-based resonance and that for many women in the United States "choice" and/or abortion access are not the most pressing feminist issues. (That "choice" is one of our greatest concerns as middle-class feminists represents of our own privileged freedom from worry about crime, class-based exploitation, welfare reform, or other feminist issues.) Further, concern arose that a march headlining "choice" would fail to acknowledge the ways in which family planning and abortion have been used to subjugate and discriminate against poor women, especially poor women of color—not only by conservative politicians and policy makers, but also by leaders within our own feminist ranks (e.g., Margaret Sanger). White, middle-class women have had the luxury of avoiding coercive contraceptive practices, let alone forced sterilizations or abortions.

In my own research on this issue,[4] I've encountered several ways in which the reproductive realities of poor women, and of poor women of color in particular, are manipulated both conspicuously and inconspicuously by the medical establishment and/or by reproductive health policies. Research participants who are poor have described doctors who, convinced the patient would be unable to take a birth-control pill everyday or use condoms consistently, pushed Norplant implants, Depo-Provera injections, or tubal ligation, sometimes even while the woman was in the throes of labor pain. These stories are a far cry from the relative reproductive autonomy of middle-class respondents, who discuss "shopping around" for the appropriate contraceptive method, and who often choose one based on noncontraceptive benefits, such as acne improvement or lighter menstrual periods. "Choice" is clearly more prominent for middle-class women than for poor women.

Lest I fail to give the pro-choice movement all the honor and gratitude it deserves (especially given my own abortion seven years ago), let me say—no, let me scream at the top of my lungs—that I still desperately want all women to have full control and autonomy over their bodies, sexuality, and reproductive destinies. I am one of millions and millions of women whose lives have been incalculably altered and improved by pro-choice feminists' efforts to avail us of contraceptive and abortion services. And, to be sure, I remain a pro-choice activist, giving time on a weekly basis to two abortion rights organizations (one national, one local). However, I have also come to believe that "choice" will only reach its truly empowering potential when we work in tandem toward reductions not just in sexism and gender inequality, but also in class- and race-based injustice, as well as in deleterious globalization processes and development policies. My hope is that, within a framework of reproductive justice, better access to sexual and reproductive health services will never trump other feminist efforts such as poverty and racism eradication, education, violence reduction, gender-sensitive development policies, fair trade, peaceful conflict resolution, and the like. Indeed, perhaps one day the movements will become so linked that we can no longer think of them as separate feminist issues.

NASAAN KA ANAK KO?
A Queer Filipina American Feminist's Tale of Abortion and Self-Recovery

PATRICIA JUSTINE TUMANG

JAMILA MAY JOSEPH IS THE NAME OF MY BIRACIAL DAUGHTER WHO was never born. She has dark brown crescent moons for eyes and a fiery tongue like her mother. Like her black Kenyan father, her skin is the color of the midnight sky. She crawls toward me on the knotted rug and smiles briefly, exposing two white knobs for teeth. Her spirit talks to me in waking dreams. I see her grow up. She learns how to walk and utters her first words. Whispering "Mama" into my ears, she rejoices in love, forgiving me again and again. Sometimes I stop seeing her, a blank space of clarity replacing memories unmade. I look in the corners and underneath the pillows. I call her name but only hear the faint gurgling of wind. I remember then that she is dead, a bloody mass of tissue flushed down the toilet. The abortion was an act of desperation. The malicious guilt never brings her back. *Nasaan ka anak ko?* Where are you, my daughter?

The name Jamila means "beautiful" in Arabic. During my senior year of college I studied abroad in Kenya for five months. While learning about Islam, Swahili civilization, and Kenyan culture, I discovered I was pregnant. George, my lover, was a Methodist black Kenyan—a rarity for the predominantly Muslim population on the Kenyan coast. I met him at a small guesthouse in Lamu where he worked as the houseboy.

When I returned to New York City after the program ended, I was nearly two months pregnant and had no financial means to support a child. My first intention was to keep the baby, so I told my middle-class Filipino mother about my pregnancy and she threatened to withdraw her financial support. I was in a bind—emotionally, spiritually, and financially. I was in a spiritual turmoil, not because of my parents' Catholic beliefs, but rather because I felt connected to the baby's spirit. But I could not envision myself giving up the middle-class privileges and lifestyle I grew up with to become a single mother and work two jobs while finishing school.

My mother and I fought about it constantly. She wanted me to finish my education and not be burdened with the responsibilities of raising a child at my age. I couldn't believe that my devoutly Catholic, Filipino mother was urging me to have an abortion. Several months after it was done, my mother revealed to me that she was pro-choice. She equated the idea of pro-choice with pro-abortion, but I understood what she was saying. I was not in a position to have the baby.

My mother never spoke to me about sexuality when I was a little girl, let alone the topic of abortion, and it was assumed I was heterosexual. When, at twenty-one, I came out to her as bisexual, she immediately dismissed me. "What do you mean," she asked, "that you are bisexual and that you are attracted to women? That's not natural!" Because she perceived heterosexuality as inherent to my sexuality, she never lost hope that someday I would meet the perfect man and reproduce for our namesake. But a poor black man from Kenya was not what she had in mind.

When I got my first period at the age of eleven, no one talked to me about my body and its development. Instead, my family made jokes about the female children and their impending womanhood. When my younger cousins had their first periods, we became the center of jokes at family reunions. Tita Leti, my father's cousin, would embarrass us during Christmastime by giving us gift-wrapped boxes of little girls' underwear. Decorated with kittens or puppies on pink or yellow cotton, my cousin, Vinci, and I dreaded the thought of wearing them. Periods, we reasoned, were a sign that we were women. Tita Leti joked with our parents, "Now you have to watch out and make sure they close their legs like good girls!" We cringed at their laughter, yet it was only in these jokes that sexuality, in heterosexual terms, was ever hinted at.

I learned about sexual development from school textbooks and discussed it with my female high-school friends, all of whom were Filipino and straight. We talked the topic of heterosexual sex to death and had unprotected sex with men. Many of my friends became pregnant and had abortions, though they didn't speak about it. They were perfect Asian girls; they couldn't. They acted calm, collected, and recovered. Until I experienced it myself, I didn't realize how much the silence burned my insides and that I too was in denial about the trauma.

My own model-minority expectations influenced my decision to have an abortion. I wasn't sure I could cope with my family and society's prejudices against my half-black child. To me, being the model minority daughter meant assimilating, speaking perfect English, adhering to a middle-class lifestyle, and establishing a successful career after college. Not being heterosexual, having a biracial baby, and being a single mother were not part of these expectations. Having internalized my parents' expectations and the United States's views on what a model minority is, I felt even more pressure to have an abortion. Not having any financial help from my mother pushed me to my final decision. I took the RU-486 pill and hoped the worst would be over.

For the next couple of weeks, I endured a living nightmare. The first dosage of Mifeprex, a medication that blocks a hormone needed for a pregnancy to continue, was given to me in pill form at the clinic. When I got home, I inserted four tablets of Misoprostol vaginally. These two medications combined to terminate the pregnancy nonsurgically. Heavy bleeding for up to two weeks was expected.

I didn't realize the horrible truth of that statement until I lay awake at night in fits of unbearable pain, bleeding through sanitary napkins by the hour. When I was in the bathroom one night, clumps of bloody tissue and embryonic remains fell into the toilet. I was overcome with tremors, my body shaking with a burst of heat resembling fever. My cheeks flushed as sweat bled into my hairline. Dragging my feet on the cold alabaster floor, I went back to bed and hid under the covers. Eyes open and bloodshot, knees to my chest, I felt tears sting my swollen cheeks. After hours of pure exhaustion, I finally fell asleep.

Returning to the clinic several days later for a scheduled follow-up, I learned that the gestational sac was still intact. I was given another dose of Mifeprex and Misoprostol. That night, I stared in horror as a clump of tissue the size of a baseball escaped from my body. I held this bloody mass in my hand, feeling the watery red liquid drip from my fingers. The tissue was soft and pliable. Poking at the flesh, I imagined the life that it embodied. The sac looked like a bleeding pig's heart. For several months after, I was unable to look at blood without vomiting.

As I was going through this experience, I remembered from my childhood the subtitled Asian movies that featured abortion scenes. In these films, the Asian female characters drank exotic herbal concoctions to terminate their pregnancies, then jumped up and down on the stairs. Scenes showed their mothers holding their hands while their fetuses became detached. In one scene, a woman in desperation took a hanger and mutilated her body, plunging rusty wires into her uterus. *Did that really happen?* I now wondered. Were those young Asian women bleeding to death? Were they real? Were they alive? How did they heal from such a trauma? Watching these images, I wondered if I could heal from my experience. Was I alone?

Deciding to have an abortion was the hardest decision I have ever made. I made it alone. Without my mother's support and in George's absence, I felt I couldn't have a child. George was very supportive despite his pro-life Christian views. Communicating through sporadic email messages and long-distance telephone calls, he said he valued my safety and saw the reality of our situation. For a moment, however, I imagined what it would be like if I could marry my poor Kenyan lover and bring him to the United States to become a family. The American Dream. George would work at a deli or be the black security guard on campus while I finished college and attained a bachelor's degree in Cultural Studies with a path in Race, Ethnicity, and Post-colonialism. I would engage him in a postmodern discourse on the white supremacist patriarchy of America and the productions of multiculturalism in the media and art, while he brought home his minimum-wage salary. Our daughter would live in a world that would exoticize and tokenize her for her kinky hair, brown skin, Asian eyes, and multilingual tongue. What does it mean that I had the capability of giving birth to new possibilities but chose to bleed her away?

I thought of my mother, a young, vibrant, and hopeful Filipina immigrant who came to America many years ago, determined to make a decent living in the land of equal opportunity. She was twenty-two years old when she gave birth to me. I was twenty-two and bleeding away. Feeling utterly dehumanized, my body an unrecognizable grotesque monster spitting out blood, I wondered about the possibility of spiritual rebirth from experiences of trauma and dehumanization. I thought of loss and survival and what this means for many of us raised among immigrant families from developing countries. I thought of my parents' transition from being working-class to middle-class and remembered clearly the losses we paid for while assimilating into a racist culture. Society gave us capital for becoming model minorities, yet systematically berated us because of our differences. We lost our mother tongue and shed our rich cultural histories as we ate hamburgers and spoke English like "true Americans."

During this time I longed to read the writings of women of color for inspiration. I scanned the libraries and searched online for feminist narratives written by women of color on abortion and found none. A majority of the books I found documented the political history of abortion, as it impacts the lives of white women. A friend suggested I read Alice Walker's *In Search Of Our Mothers' Gardens*. Choking on tears, I read about Walker's abortion in the mid–1960s when she returned to the United States from a trip to Africa. She had been a senior in college and discovered that she was pregnant, alone, and penniless. Thinking of Walker's time, when safe and legal abortions were a privilege, I counted my blessings and buried my pain into the depths of me, far from eyes that see, to a solitary place where whispers mingle and collide in silence.

In the culture of silence that was pervasive in my Filipino household, children—particularly little girls—were not allowed to speak unless spoken to. I learned at an early age the art of keeping silent. I knew to keep quiet when my father's expression became stern and a hardened thin line formed on his forehead like a frowning wrinkle. All the pains, the joys, and the heartaches of my life festered inside me, creating gaping wounds between the silences. My tongue was a well, containing words fit to burst and flood the Pacific Ocean. Yet only English came out. In short. And polite. Sentences. At home and abroad we sang in English, raged in English, loved and dreamed in English.

As a child I found unexplainable joy in singing Tagalog songs that I had learned by listening to my parents' Filipino audio tapes given to us by visiting relatives. They were played only on special occasions. Although I couldn't understand a word, I sang unabashedly. The act of singing Tagalog was dangerous and daring. Rooted in a desperate aching to speak a language other than English, I felt like a mischievous child stealing a cookie from the forbidden cookie jar, and I slowly savored every bite. In this hunger I realized the power of voice even while I couldn't speak. At a later age, I realized writing was another way to emerge from the silence into a place of healing.

I looked to writing as a means for what black feminist writer bell hooks has termed "self-recovery." I wrote for survival about the physical and emotional abuse I experienced as a child in a sexist household. And later, I wrote to recover from my traumatic abortion. I found strength in the words of Alice Walker, Cherríe Moraga, Nellie Wong, Audre Lorde, Lois-Ann Yamanaka, Gloria Anzaldúa, Maxine Hong Kingston, Angela Y. Davis, and Mitsuye Yamada. I read until my vision was a blur. The battles and writings of these women inspired me to heal. I too wanted to break the silence.

When considering abortion options, my friends in New York had encouraged me to take RU-486. They told me it would be an easier, quieter trauma. Finding information on the pill wasn't difficult. It was introduced to the American market in September 2000 but had been available in Europe for many years. I conducted online research and realized I had to make a quick decision. It was only prescribed to women who were less than seven weeks pregnant, and I was a budding eight weeks. RU-486 appealed to me because it had an effiicacy rate of 99 percent and was non-surgical. I contacted a small primary healthcare clinic in Brooklyn that offered the pill for women up to nine weeks pregnant. It was the same price as a surgical abortion and was advertised as being "less traumatic." According to my research, RU-486 was given commendable reviews by women who had tried it.

If I had known how traumatic my experience with RU-486 would be, I would have opted for the surgical method. Not that it would have been less traumatic, but anything would have been better than the three weeks of horrendous bleeding and cramping I endured. My friends' support helped me through the difficult moments, but those who had urged me to take the pill had known nothing about it. Those who had had surgical abortions just thought the pill would be easier by comparison. The doctor who had prescribed it to me told me that although she had never taken it, she had heard that the procedure was only slightly uncomfortable. I had no adequate aftercare or education about the side effects, except what was written in small print on the pamphlets I was given. My doctor had informed me that all the information I needed to know was right there. I felt so terrifyingly alone in the process.

Much of the pro-life debate in the United States has centered on the protection of life. Not just any life, but the lives of white babies. Reproductive rights are not just white women's issues. When I researched abortion costs at various clinics in New York, I found that only a few provide a sliding-scale option. The *Roe v. Wade* decision granted the right to abortion but not the access. The time has more than arrived to discuss the racism, classism, homophobia, and heterosexism of some doctors and clinicians regarding abortion and healthcare. I align myself with the pro-choice movement, but that does not mean I advocate abortion. Instead, I believe women of all backgrounds should have the right to a clean and safe abortion by a licensed practitioner if that is their choice.

Healing eventually came from actively talking about my abortion with my mother and friends. Whether through speech or writing, it meant consciously remembering the experience. It meant talking about how our bodies have never been our own. For centuries we have been controlled, sterilized, and raped by masculine, imperialist, and white supremacist forces. The predominantly white and racist feminist movement of the 1970s ignored the relationship between racism, sexism, classism, and homophobia. I know intimately how this pervasive feminist thinking has denied the complexities of the oppressions I fight in my daily life. In the growing emergence of "third-wave" feminism, we know that feminism isn't reduced to one English-speaking white face from North America. Asian American feminists must not remain invisible in the feminist struggle, because we too are angry at the injustices that we face in this country. We yearn for a feminism that addresses our realities as Asian American women and women of color, one that incorporates race, class, gender, and sexuality in its analysis. We long for a feminism that addresses the struggle of reproductive rights for women of color in the United States as well as in the third world.

Even for those who can afford to get an abortion, in my experience there has been a serious lack of education about procedures and proper emotional and physical aftercare. While some women have had positive experiences with RU-486, mine was not one of them. Almost a year after the abortion, the pain still visited me from time to time. For so long, I tried to deny that I had undergone a traumatic experience, and I entered a period of self-punishment. I pretended to be recovered, but the pain pushed itself outward. Regret and guilt caused severe anxiety attacks that left me breathless, convulsing, and faint.

When I returned to the clinic after the abortion, I was told I needed therapy for my depression and anxiety. A white female doctor began asking questions about me, my family, and my refusal to seek therapy. I suggested that I join a support group for women of color who had abortions and was informed by the doctor that there were none, to her knowledge, in New York City. She asked me why I would feel more comfortable around other women of color and not a white man. I felt extremely uncomfortable by her questioning, and she pressed on, a few words short of calling me a separatist. Since my own abortion, I have realized that women of color need access to post-abortion therapy that is affordable, accessible, and sensitive to different cultures and sexualities.

To fully heal, I ultimately have had to let go. I didn't let go of the memory but of this imaginary noose that restrained me and kept me from self-love. I hadn't learned as a child to love myself. Rather, I had been taught to be a good Filipina girl and do as I was told. This noose now came in the forms of denial, self-punishment, and attracting unsupportive people in my life. I also had to take some time away from my mother to retreat from her anger and hurt to process my own. The first few months after the abortion we didn't speak that often. Eventually I entered therapy, which my mother paid for out of guilt, despite our emotional distance. Talking about my abortion with another woman of color proved a relief. I found support and a safe space to open up.

My mother eventually broke down. She called in tears and apologized for not supporting me during my ordeal. I knew in my heart that if I was to forgive myself, I must also forgive her. She too was wounded and realized that she would not have known what to do in my situation. I felt closer to her at that point.

Healing has never been as easy process for me. Something always interrupts it. New relationships, disagreements with family or friends, old issues, work, and school. Denial coats the pain and prevents actual healing. When I become scared of my emotions and feel buried, I remember to love myself and know that I am not alone. I struggle with my inner demons constantly. Although I am only in the beginning stages of my healing process, I feel that I have now entered a place of peace. Regret does nothing to change things. Although my decision was difficult, I made the best choice for my circumstances. It is my daughter's spirit that calls me out of grief. In my insistence on remembering her, I have found healing. She comes to me in dreams and comforts me during difficult times. She gives me a vision for the future where there is love instead of suffering. A place where there is healing from dehumanization. I struggle for her vision everyday.

A NEW VISION FOR ADVANCING OUR MOVEMENT FOR REPRODUCTIVE HEALTH, REPRODUCTIVE RIGHTS, AND REPRODUCTIVE JUSTICE

ASIAN COMMUNITIES FOR REPRODUCTIVE JUSTICE

Reproductive justice is important because it tells us the truth about our bodies, our lives, our families, our world.

FOUNDED IN 1989, ASIAN COMMUNITIES FOR REPRODUCTIVE Justice (ACRJ) has been at the forefront of building a Reproductive Justice Movement that places the reproductive health and rights of Asian women and girls within a social-justice framework. We are committed, as part of the Reproductive Justice Movement, to exploring and articulating the intersection of racism, sexism, xenophobia, heterosexism, and class oppression in women's lives. ACRJ is a founding member of the SisterSong Women of Color Reproductive Health Collective, which uses the reproductive justice framework as its central organizing strategy in the protection of women's human rights in resistance to reproductive oppression.

HISTORICAL CONTEXT

The fight for women's liberation has been inextricably linked to control over reproduction; nevertheless, birth control has also been used as a tool of women's oppression. For example, in the early twentieth century, the eugenics movement began to promote policies that restricted reproduction of society's most marginalized communities, and adopted access to birth control in order to achieve population control. Thus birth control was used to exert further control over individuals and communities that were already facing multiple oppressions. As movements for women's rights have evolved, the dialogue concerning reproduction control has also changed dramatically over time, resulting in the creation of the reproductive health, reproductive rights, and reproductive justice frameworks.

Though highly problematic from an antiracist and anti-imperialist perspective, population-control discourse was politically successful in increasing the visibility and acceptance of birth control in the first half of the twentieth century. At the same time, African American women who made connections between race, class, and gender joined the fight for birth control in the 1920s, as much from black women's experience as enslaved breeders for the accumulation of wealth of white slave-owners as for the realization of gender empowerment. In the 1960s, the U.S. federal government began funding family planning in the United States and internationally as part of a strategy for population control, rather than women's empowerment. Population control has been defined as externally imposed efforts by governments, corporations, or private agencies to control (by increasing or limiting) population growth, usually by controlling women's reproduction and fertility.[1] Other forms of population control include immigration restrictions, selective population movement or dispersal, incarceration, and various forms of discrimination.

As an outgrowth of the civil rights and women's liberation movements, the women's health movement of the 1970s established women-centered health clinics throughout the country to provide access to family planning and reproductive health services. There was a strong focus on abortion rights, culminating with the landmark 1973 decision in *Roe v. Wade* that legalized abortion nationwide. The *Roe v. Wade* decision struck down state laws that had previously outlawed abortion, making the procedure more accessible and safe, and set a precedent for numerous other subsequent cases. Explaining the link between social and economic participation and reproduction, the Supreme Court noted in *Planned Parenthood of Southeastern Pennsylvania v. Casey*[2] in 1992 that "the ability of women to participate equally in the economic and social life of the Nation has been facilitated by their ability to control their reproductive lives."

The reproductive rights framework came to champion women's entitlement to a full range of rights related to reproduction, reproductive freedom, and reproductive health. However, by the 1990s, there was wide recognition by women's advocates that an approach combining resistance to population control and advocacy for abortion rights was too narrow to achieve the larger goal of women's empowerment.

OPPRESSION AND REPRODUCTION

If I could describe myself in one word, it would be "courageous."
—ACRJ Youth Activist

Reproductive oppression is the controlling and exploiting of women and girls through our bodies, our sexuality, and our reproduction (both biological and social) by families, communities, institutions, and society.

Reproduction encompasses both the biological and social processes related to conception, birth, nurturing, and raising of children as participants in society. *Social reproduction* is the reproduction of society, which includes the reproduction of roles, such as race, class, and gender roles.

Both the reproductive health and reproductive rights frameworks largely focus on individual rights and solutions rather than structural societal changes. Many of the women who are most oppressed and at the margins of the movements for reproductive autonomy have championed the need for greater analysis of oppression in discussions of reproduction. The existing discourse and focus of the reproductive health and rights agenda rarely includes an analysis of the effects of intersecting forms of oppression. When racial analysis has been inserted into mainstream discourse, it has often used a black-and-white framework without integrating the racial oppression experienced by Asian and Pacific Islander (API), Latina, Indigenous, Arab, and Middle Eastern women. The focus on and orientation toward individual rights and individual responsibility (as they relate to articulation of reproductive health and women's choice) reinforces the broader systems of political, economic, and cultural hegemony that maintain racial stratification—primarily through white supremacy—in the United States.

Examples of reproductive injustice abound in the United States and in the world. The control of black women's fertility during slavery, as well as via current welfare-reform policies, is key to racial stigmatization and economic oppression of the black community. Historical sterilization abuse in Native American communities was part of a genocidal strategy of decimation. Similarly, women with disabilities have been targeted for coerced sterilization and fertility control, and Puerto Rican women were also sterilized in large numbers. Additionally, with an eye to limiting poor populations, contraceptives such as Depo-Provera and Norplant, which are potentially dangerous if used long term, are systematically pushed on poor and young women of color in the United States. In each case, an imperialist agenda to secure land, resources, and women's labor has led to control over the bodies of women of color.

Repeatedly, economic, social, and institutional policies have severely affected women's choice to determine their reproduction. The regulation and control of API's women and girls' bodies, sexuality, and reproduction have played a key role in colonization and racial oppression, and in controlling API communities in the United States. Historically, the nation's immigrant exclusion laws targeted people from Asia and served as a form of population control. As early as 1870, in an attempt to limit the size of the Asian population in California, the state legislature passed a law that prohibited the immigration of Asian women, and in 1875, the U.S. Congress passed the Page Law to forbid entry of mostly "Chinese, Japanese, and Mongolian" women. Current policies restricting immigration and access to social services also significantly prevent API women from truly being able to make reproductive choices. For example, API women who speak limited English and who access welfare payments often do not have a complete picture of their rights and status, and are unable to advocate for themselves or navigate the complex bureaucratic system because of the lack of sufficient interpreters. Moreover, though the use of the pesticide DDT is banned in the continental United States, over the past forty years American corporations have dumped vast amounts of agricultural chemicals, including DDT, in Hawaii; mounting evidence suggests that these pesticides play a role in breast cancer development. Today, native Hawaiians have one of the highest breast cancer rates in the world.[3]

Women of color, including API women, face oppression not only due to their gender, but also for many other reasons. The long history of colonization and Western imperialism have institutionalized racism, xenophobia, heterosexism, and class oppression in this society so that policies supposedly designed to serve all women often function to perpetuate injustice for women of color. For instance, immigrant or refugee

API women with limited English proficiency have little power to negotiate interactions with reproductive health providers.

In addition to race and class discrimination, many API queer women and transgender people face homophobia that deters them from accessing reproductive care. Reproductive health programs and service providers often focus on women as individuals and may adopt a paternalistic approach that oppresses and regulates women's reproduction. Although there is currently a movement to incorporate cultural competence and language access in health services, these interventions usually do not address power differential in the patient-provider relationship. They do not empower API women to be partners with medical practitioners. Also, they usually do not incorporate or respect traditional health practices that API women value, such as homeopathic medicine, herbal healing, or acupuncture. Without an intersectional analysis of the impact of multiple forms of oppression, the reproductive health and rights movements' focus on individual health and choice poses challenges and limitations as a framework for achieving reproductive justice for API women.

As Dorothy Roberts eloquently stated, "Reproduction is not just a matter of individual choice. Reproductive health policy affects the status of entire groups. It reflects which people are valued in our society; who is deemed worthy to bear children and capable of making decisions for themselves. Reproductive decisions are made within a social context, including inequalities of wealth and power."[4] The focus on individualism neglects the broader societal context in which API women live.

API women's reproductive options and ability to control their reproductive lives are limited in many ways. For refugee women who have survived war in their home countries, oppression is often enacted on their bodies. During war, a woman's body is treated synonymously with the land: It's a battleground where women and resources are exploited, a site where victors establish dominance by reproducing themselves in the population through women's bodies, as well as reproducing the victors' values, culture, religion, language, and traditions. In addition to being more susceptible to HIV/AIDS, reproductive tract infections (RTIs), sexually transmitted diseases (STDs), and other health risks, and having limited access to healthcare, women trafficked from poor countries such as Thailand, Cambodia, and the Philippines are more vulnerable to physical abuse and suffer a range of mental and emotional trauma. They also often lack access to language tools and legal help, and thus are trapped in a state of powerlessness. These are just some of the concrete examples of how reproductive justice is central to API women's struggle for self-determination.

In focusing on a narrow abortion agenda, or even a broader reproductive health agenda, the reproductive health and reproductive rights frameworks may neglect critical circumstances many API women face. API women experiencing poverty, linguistic isolation, domestic violence, human trafficking, and harsh working conditions are focused on survival and do not have the luxury of "choice" because their options are limited. In addition, the focus on individualism does not speak to the experiences of API women. Numerous cultures across Asia promote societal, community, and family decision-making that is incompatible with individualistic reproductive rights. In making reproductive decisions, API women often have to navigate social taboos and traditions within their own cultures, so the "choice" is not necessarily theirs to make.

CREATION OF THE WOMEN OF COLOR REPRODUCTIVE JUSTICE MOVEMENT

Reproductive justice, as defined by ACRJ, will be achieved when women and girls have the economic, social, and political power and resources to make healthy decisions about their bodies, sexuality, and reproduction, for themselves, their families and their communities in all areas of their lives.

In resistance to reproductive oppression, women of color in the United States and internationally have long advocated for a broader reproductive justice analysis that addresses race, class, gender, sexuality, ability, age, and immigration status.

In many countries, the term "sexual health and rights" is used to describe an analogous constellation of reproductive justice issues. Issues of sexual health and rights include sexual violence against women; comprehensive sex education; marriage rights, including same-sex marriage; and sexual torture during wartime. Current government policies throughout the world attempt to control sexual relations among people.[5] Sexual health and rights advocates proclaim that humans are sexual by nature[6] and thereby make the connection between sexual rights and human rights. According to the Platform for Action of the Fourth World Conference on Women in Beijing, "the human rights of women include their right to have control over and decide freely and responsibly matters related to their sexuality."[7] Activists call for government to ensure that "public and economic policies, and public services and education, prevent discrimination and abuse in relation to sexuality and promote sexual health and rights."[8]

Although some historians have tended to erase the contributions of women of color, ACRJ has been actively organizing for reproductive justice for many years. In the past two decades, this race- and ethnicity-based organizing has gained visibility and increasing success. The National Black Women's Health Project was formed in 1984 as the first women-of-color reproductive health organization, building a foundation for women-of-color organizations representing the United States' major ethnic groups. The Mother's Milk Project on the Akwesasne Reservation in New York was founded in 1985, followed by the National Latina Health Organization in 1986. The Native American Women's Health Education and Resource Center was launched in 1988, and Asian Pacific Islanders for Choice (a forerunner to ACRJ) appeared in 1989. Since then, women of color have organized numerous conferences, established myriad organizations, collaborated with each other, and formed alliances with civil rights and women's rights organizations.

In November 1994, a Black women's caucus first coined the term "reproductive justice," naming themselves Women of African Descent for Reproductive Justice at the Illinois Pro-Choice Alliance Conference. According to Loretta Ross, one of the caucus participants:

> "We were dissatisfied with the pro-choice language, feeling that it did not adequately encompass our twin goals: To protect the right to have—and to not have—children. Nor did the language of choice accurately portray the many barriers African American women faced when trying to make reproductive decisions. Perhaps because we were just returning from the International Conference on Population and Development in Cairo, Egypt, in 1994, we began exploring the use of the human rights framework in our reproductive rights activism in the United States, as many grassroots activists do globally. We sought a way to partner reproductive rights with social justice and came up with the term 'reproductive justice.'"[9]

A few years later, in 1997, the SisterSong Women of Color Reproductive Health Collective was formed by sixteen women-of-color organizations, with a focus on grassroots mobilization and public policy. SisterSong began popularizing the term "reproductive justice" based on the human rights framework. In April 2004, SisterSong coordinated women-of-color groups to mobilize thousands of women in a Women of Color for Reproductive Justice contingent as part of the March for Women's Lives in Washington, D.C. And in October 2004, the groundbreaking book *Undivided Rights: Women of Color Organize for Reproductive Justice* (South End Press, 2004) provided a comprehensive history of women of color organizing around reproductive health, reproductive rights, and reproductive justice issues, documenting their vital contributions which hitherto had been largely unreported.

ATTACKING REPRODUCTIVE OPPRESSION: ACRJ'S REPRODUCTIVE JUSTICE AGENDA

A political struggle that does not have women at the heart of it, above it, below it, and within it is no struggle at all.

—Arundhati Roy

When I think about how others struggled to give us rights and privileges now, it means a lot to me and I'm very thankful.

—ACRJ Youth Activist

At ACRJ, we work toward a vision of the world where Asian women and girls have self-determination, power, and resources to make their own decisions. Our vision requires that women, girls, and their communities have all they need to thrive, creating an environment for personal, collective, and societal transformation.

Through our reproductive justice analysis work, we host discussion and strategy sessions to deepen and broaden our analysis. We write and disseminate articles to build the base of the movement, and have developed a reproductive justice agenda that informs and directs our work. Our reproductive justice agenda illustrates our vision, solutions, and guiding principles for attacking the root causes of reproductive oppression. In this agenda we articulate our analysis based on the lived experiences, issues, and research carried out for and by Asian women and girls to develop a model that addresses the nexus of systems of oppression based on gender, race, class, sexuality, ability, age, and immigration status. We use popular education and community-based participatory research to develop the leadership of Asian women and girls to plan and lead campaigns to achieve specific and measurable gains at the local and state levels. For instance, we worked in collaboration with environmental justice groups to shut down a toxic medical waste incinerator in Oakland, California, and have been working to pass and enforce state legislation that ensures comprehensive sex education in public high schools. In our commitment to advancing the Reproductive Justice Movement, we build and strengthen women-of-color and mainstream alliances for reproductive justice. We recognize the importance of broader inclusion and leadership of the most excluded groups of women. These include low-income women, queer women, transgender individuals, women with disabilities, young women, and immigrant and refugee women. We believe that organized communities, particularly the most marginalized groups mentioned above, are key agents of change, and we focus on improving social conditions and changing power and access to resources on all levels.

ACRJ's reproductive justice agenda (RJA) places reproductive justice at the center of the most critical social and economic justice issues facing our communities, such as ending violence against women, workers' rights, environmental justice, queer rights, immigrant rights, and educational justice, which have major implications for Asian women. For example, under conditions of reproductive justice, we will live in homes free from sexual and physical violence; we will live and work without fear of sexual harassment; we will have safe work and home environments protected from corporate exploitation and environmental toxins; we will be free from hatred due to sexual identity; we will be valued for all the forms of work we do; we will earn equitable and livable wages; we will eat healthy and affordable food; and we will have comprehensive healthcare for ourselves and our families. Moreover, the government and private institutions will support our decisions around whether or not to have a child, and we will receive the necessary support for our choices. In addition, we will receive an education that honors and teaches the contributions of women, people of color, working-class communities, and queer and transgender communities.

Women's bodies, reproduction, and sexuality are often used as the excuse and the target for unequal treatment in the attempt to control our communities. We believe that by challenging patriarchal social relations and addressing the intersection of racism, sexism, xenophobia, homophobia, and class oppression within a women-of-color context, we will be able to build the collective social, economic, and political power of all women and girls to make decisions that protect and contribute to our reproductive health and overall well-being. From this vision, we have developed key strategies and projects that enable ACRJ to have an impact on the grassroots, community, state, and national levels. From the perspective of a reproductive justice framework, the key problem is a lack of power, resources, and control.

TRANSLATING VISION INTO ACTION: ACRJ'S IMPACT

Efforts to advance reproductive justice cannot be achieved by vision and analysis alone. In our work with Asian women and girls in California, we have translated our vision for reproductive justice into specific gains at the local and state levels, which include the following:

Developing New Leaders

In line with our vision, we believe those who are directly impacted by reproductive oppression must be at the forefront of leading and making change. Since 1998, ACRJ has instituted a youth organizing program involving over 250 low-income, young Asian women across California. These young women receive intensive leadership development, popular education, and organizing training to become effective leaders and powerful organizers for reproductive and social justice. A cadre of underserved girls from immigrant and refugee families, comprehensively trained on essential issues of reproductive health and their connection to poverty, education, and employment represents a real first, not only for the local community, but also for this portion of the national Asian population.

Campaigning for and Advancing the Reproductive Justice of Asian Women and Girls.

By organizing for specific gains, youth activists have won campaigns protecting the reproductive health of Asian women. For example, the Healthy Communities Campaign, in collaboration with environmental justice groups, increased the visibility of reproductive health issues related to toxic emissions and culminated in victory when one of the most toxic medical-waste incinerators in the nation was forced to close in 2002.

Educating Community Leaders

ACRJ youth organizers created the Reproductive Freedom Tour of Oakland and accompanying guidebook to educate researchers, community members, and policy makers on the issues impacting their community. The tour focuses on reproductive and social justice issues such as welfare, educational justice, and gentrification.

Addressing the Language Needs of Immigrant and Refugee Asian Communities

ACRJ youth leaders conducted surveys in Mien, Cambodian, Cantonese, and English to assess the impact of welfare reform and the true needs of community members, and discovered that the biggest barrier facing immigrant women was the lack of interpreters at the Department of Social Services. This effort culminated in the first-ever Southeast Asian *community forum* in which ACRJ members educated staff at the Department of Social Services about the need for appropriate interpreters and translation for clients.

Advocating for Comprehensive Sexuality Education in California Public Schools

Over the past few years, ACRJ has partnered with the ACLU of Northern California to pass and enforce SB 71, which simplifies sex-education guidelines and ensures that public-school sexuality education is comprehensive, accurate, and free of bias. ACRJ has been conducting youth and adult training across California to ensure that communities are aware of the new law and that they have the tools to hold schools accountable as needed.

Researching for Toxins in Personal-Care Products

Asian women and girls are affected by personal-care product chemicals in a myriad of ways—through personal use promoted by marketing trends, through occupational exposures that are facilitated by poverty and immigrant status, and through hazardous exposures and the lack of access to healthcare. In response to the wide body of evidence that shows the health hazards of beauty products, ACRJ has established POLISH, the Participatory Research, Organizing, and Leadership Initiative for Safety and Health. POLISH participants are currently researching the degree to which Asian women and girls—and the many Asian women who work in nail salons—are exposed to toxic chemicals through both personal use and professional occupation. The results will fill major gaps in information, and the project will increase Asian girls' and women's capacity to identify reproductive justice problems and intervene in their community's health status.

The ultimate goal of our work is to build self-determination for individuals and communities. For reproductive justice to be real, change needs to be made at all levels of society. We believe that translating the vision of our reproductive justice agenda into action will bring about change on the individual, community, institutional, and societal levels in order to transform our world:

1.   Individual women and girls will acquire skills as well as demonstrate leadership and commitment to furthering reproductive justice;

2.   Communities will change attitudes and behaviors to support women and girls as community leaders;

3.   Institutions, such as churches, schools and their districts; businesses and workplaces; or legislative bodies, will make changes to stop reproductive oppression and protect reproductive justice for women and girls; and

4.   Women and girls will gain complete self-determination and all forms of oppression will end.

Reproductive justice means learning about your body, your talents, your strengths, and empowering yourself.

—ACRJ Youth Activist

WHERE DO WE GO FROM HERE?

We are currently in a time of increasing instability, violence, and consolidation of state and corporate power in the United States and around the world. These conditions provide fertile ground for an escalated assault on women's reproductive justice. The war in Iraq, new appointments to the Supreme Court that promise to swing the court to the Right, cuts to public assistance, the continued erosion of abortion access and reproductive healthcare, the passage of anti-immigrant and anti-youth legislation, and weakening environmental policies that allow toxins to contaminate our bodies and food supplies exemplify the strength and comprehensiveness of these attacks on the self-determination of women and our communities.

Moreover, mainstream reproductive rights leaders acknowledge that the movement is shrinking. By integrating the reproductive justice needs of our communities at local, state, national, and international levels, we will be able to activate and mobilize larger constituencies. If our movement is fresh and relevant, it will flourish rather than diminish.

By organizing our communities, we create space for women and girls to be active and full agents of change in their lives. Reproductive justice empowers women and girls to fully come into their strong, talented selves by creating environments in which they feel loved, safe, powerful, and confident. Reproductive justice builds community among women and girls and creates opportunities for rich discussion where they can work out the conflicting messages they receive about complex issues such as identity, sexuality, and power.

We need a movement with a vision for addressing women wholly and comprehensively, so that we do not single out pieces of a woman's body, but see their bodies as whole. Similarly, we cannot focus solely on one aspect of a woman's life, whether at work, at school, at home, or on the streets. We need to understand how reproductive oppression may exist in all arenas of her life, and recognize that she may have to walk through all of these arenas in a single day.

Reproductive justice calls for integrated analysis, holistic vision, and comprehensive strategies that push against the structural and societal conditions that control our communities by regulating our bodies, sexuality, and reproduction. This is the time to come together across separate identities, issue areas, and change efforts to achieve the vision that will enable all women, girls, and communities to truly transform our world.

> *It is time to speak your Truth. Create your community. And do not look outside yourself for the leader. We are the ones we have been waiting for.*
> —*Hopi Elder, activist*

HELP US ADVANCE REPRODUCTIVE JUSTICE

Here are several ways you can help build a shared vision of reproductive justice to guide substantive work in our communities and beyond.

These suggestions serve simply as starting points to inspire your own activism and as opportunities for advancing our movement:

Reproductive Rights and Parental-Consent Laws

Few would disagree that it is better when young people communicate with their parents in deciding whether or not to have an abortion. With the mandating of parental notification, however, some teenagers may choose to have unsafe and illegal abortions, delay seeking medical care, or travel out of state if they are forced to either face a judge or unsupportive parents, thus greatly increasing their physical and emotional health risks.

What You Can Do

- Organize and educate women, girls, and their families, not only about access to abortion for young women, but also its connection to other reproductive justice and social justice issues.
- Strengthen alliances and coalitions with social justice groups who traditionally do not work in reproductive justice but whose constituencies are or will be deeply impacted by the issue. By working with the community and in coalition, build a strong base with long-term capacity, leadership, and electoral power.
- In partnership with state coalitions such as the Campaign for Teen Safety in California, advocate for upholding reproductive rights for women of all ages and preserving safety for teenagers.
- Ensure the healthcare system provides resources, information, and quality care to women and teenagers about their reproductive choices.

Queer and Transgender Rights and Healthcare Bias

For queer women and transgender individuals, access to healthcare is often limited by bias and discrimination in the medical community, delayed medical care, and a lack of research on healthcare needs and risks.

Queer women and transgender people must have the ability to exercise self-determination over their identity and their sexual lives as well as full civil rights, free from discrimination and harassment.

What You Can Do

- Organize efforts to incorporate queer and transgender-friendly healthcare programs into mainstream hospitals and clinics, public agencies, and community organizations in order to create a safer and more responsive environment.
- Support enforcement of California's new law that bans denial of insurance coverage based on transgender status and adds gender and gender identity to existing antidiscrimination provisions in state laws regulating insurance companies and healthcare plans (AB 1586).
- Advocate for marriage equality, the legal recognition of same-sex marriage, which affords full federal and state benefits.
- Oppose any federal and state efforts that write discrimination into the constitution.

Educational Justice and Comprehensive Sexuality Education

Medically accurate, age-appropriate, comprehensive sexuality education is essential for the healthy development of young people and their relationships with each other. Research shows that by combining an abstinence message with information about condoms and contraception, as well as communication and refusal skills, comprehensive sex education is effective for improving young peoples' understanding of themselves and their health, and preventing teen pregnancy and STI transmission.[10]

What You Can Do

- Mobilize parents, family members, and community members in your neighborhood to research and develop a "report card" that assesses the state of sexuality education in your local school district.

- Hold school boards and school administrators accountable for providing comprehensive sex education in public schools.
- Support state and federal legislation that mandates, enforces, and provides resources for comprehensive sexuality education, such as the federal Responsible Education About Life Act (SB 368) and the Family Life Education Act (HR 768).

Environmental Justice and Personal-Care Products

Women and girls are exposed to hazardous chemicals on a consumer level through their personal-care products, and on an occupational level through work in the beauty industry. Lacking Food and Drug Administration regulation, only 11 percent of more than 10,500 ingredients in personal-care products have been tested for safety thus far.[11] Some of the toxins in beauty products are endocrine disruptors, which interfere with the normal functioning of hormones, and all of the toxins are associated with reproductive, developmental, and other health problems.

What You Can Do

- Pressure the FDA to regulate personal care products, and the personal-care products industry to manufacture products without toxins. For instance, the Campaign for Safe Cosmetics works to mandate the phasing-out of chemicals that are known to cause or are suspected of causing cancer, genetic mutation, or reproductive harm (www.safecosmetics.org). African American Women Evolving's Healthy Vagina Campaign informs women of the potential risks associated with douching and advocates for stricter regulation of manufacturers of feminine-hygiene products.

- Organize and educate women consumers and workers about the health hazards of toxins in personal-care products.
- Support enforcement of California's new law that calls for the full disclosure of ingredients known to cause cancer or birth defects and investigation of the health impacts of these chemicals (SB 484).
- Advocate for legislative proposals that will ban these toxic chemicals entirely in cosmetics and other personal-care products.

Workers' Rights and Undocumented Women Laborers

Undocumented women laborers in the electronics industry, garment industry, and domestic services industry are burdened with low wages, little (if any) access to healthcare, and substandard working conditions. Moreover, these immigrant and refugee workers are vulnerable to abuse and exploitation from employers who would deny them the few rights they might have.

What You Can Do

- In your local community, develop efforts to establish workers' centers or worker cooperatives that provide a safe and central place for workers to receive training, support, referrals, and resources.
- Encourage unions to be increasingly supportive of their growing immigrant base and more active in fighting for immigrant and refugee workers' rights.
- Join an organization that leads campaigns to protect the rights of undocumented women workers, such as CAAAV Organizing Asian Communities, which organizes across immigrant, working-class, and poor Asian communities (www.caaav.org); Sweatshop Watch, which works to eliminate exploitation and inhumane conditions that characterize sweatshops (www.sweatshopwatch.org); and Asian Immigrant Women Advocates, which empowers low-income,

immigrant women workers to make change in their workplaces, communities, and broader society (www.aiwa.org).

- Support legislative efforts to advance workers' rights for undocumented women laborers.

Ending Violence Against Women and Human Trafficking

The lucrative industry of trafficking women and children for the purposes of manual and/or sexual labor is finally being revealed as the crisis it is. The fight against trafficking, and consequent indentured servitude and prostitution, involves empowering those whose age, gender, poverty, and national origin make them a target for exploitation, as well as addressing the structural causes which allow it to flourish.

What You Can Do

- Expose the hidden industry of human trafficking through increased awareness, knowledge, and research.
- Join campaigns that work to fight trafficking, such as Gabriela Network's Purple Rose Campaign, which works to create an international movement against the sex trafficking of Filipina women and their children (www.gabnet.org).
- Organize a coalition of service providers, public health workers, trafficked women and girls, and community members to inform, educate and mobilize people in your area.
- Lobby for local, state, and federal regulations and enforcement that prevent women and girls from being trafficked, and prosecute traffickers, including implementation of two California laws (AB 22 and SB 180).

Immigrant Rights and Exclusion and Discrimination

Xenophobic laws and attitudes in the United States mean that immigrant activists and communities are continually fighting a reactionary battle. The specter of immigration raids, vigilante groups, detentions, deportations, and family separations can prevent women and families from seeking needed social services to ensure that their communities continue to grow and thrive.

What You Can Do

- Support immigrant and refugee leaders to lead national debates and counter xenophobic public attitudes. Build the base of immigrants, refugees, and allies who organize on the local and national levels to protect and expand the rights of immigrants, regardless of immigration status.
- Sign up for the Immigrant Rights News sponsored by the National Network for Immigrant and Refugee Rights, which works to promote a just immigration and refugee policy and defend and expand immigrant and refugee rights in the United States (www.nnirr.org).
- Fight legislative and ballot proposals that aim to perpetuate discrimination and exclusion against immigrant communities.
- Support comprehensive immigration reform that will reunite families, protect workers, and bring stability to the lives of immigrants and refugees, such as the Save America Comprehensive Immigration Act of 2005 (HR 2092).

WE HAVE MET THE ENEMY, AND SHE/HE IS US

MARGARET R. JOHNSTON

We are all of us responsible for our myriad pollutions; public, private and political.

—Walt Kelly, Creator of *Pogo*[1]

I WAS JUST A YOUNG PUP WHEN THE *POGO* CARTOON THAT contained this line was published. As kids, my brothers and I loved the iconoclastic bunch of philosophizing animal misfits who lived in Okefenokee Swamp. It was mostly political satire, and we could figure out which characters were really J. Edgar Hoover, Spiro Agnew, Joe McCarthy (Simple J. Malarkey), and others who today's readers might translate to Rumsfeld, Cheney, or "Condi." But this line—*We have met the enemy, and he is us*—was about our treatment of the environment, and this cartoon ran in celebration of the first Earth Day in 1970.

Oh, I remember thinking, *it's not just about how the leaders mess things up, it's about what we all do.* It's hard to take responsibility for what's wrong in a culture; we think that social change is something that exists outside of us instead of a result of what we do or say or think. I count *Pogo* as one of my early influences and I think it is worth looking at what power *we all* have to move the current logjam of public opinion about abortion.

Before I hear someone from the pro-choice camp protest that we didn't create this mess, I want to give full credit to the anti-abortion movement for succeeding in stigmatizing abortion. All that standing in front of abortion clinics and screaming at young women, "Don't kill your baby!" and "Mommy, don't murder me!" has really paid off. Today it is the rare woman presenting herself for an abortion who has not debated those picketers in her head. Terrorism is just as effective in Birmingham, Alabama,[2] as it is in Baghdad. Most doctors and healthcare workers involved in abortion care have to at least grapple with whether they could become the target of some nut who wants to kill them. As for the politicians, they don't need to think, they only need to *fear* electoral defeat at the hands of the well-organized fundamentalist troops that get whipped up over opposing abortion. The populace has not been so polarized about a social issue since the McCarthy era. There are such negative cultural messages about abortion that 47 percent of women in a large study said that they feel stigmatized by having an abortion. In other words, they think that if someone knew they had an abortion, that person would think less of them.[3]

It would be easy to say, "It's all the fault of fundamentalist anti-abortion fanatics," and do a righteous, angry counterprotest next time the January 22 *Roe v. Wade* anniversary rolls around. But we are not fighting the "antis"; we are fighting ignorance, intolerance, and injustice. It is too easy to join the fray of the "Abortion War" and forget that the path to peace and understanding may be more within our control than we think. As an abortion provider, I have been *toe-to-toe* with anti abortion activists, and I am here to say that facing off against the anti-abortion movement only feeds it. It needs our participation in the Abortion War to have someone to play the bad guy to its "rescuer."[4] Although this may not work everywhere, I have found that when I stopped yelling at the protesters, they stopped coming to my clinic. The constant polarization of the abortion issue has the effect of draining valuable energy from the women and men who need it, and silencing well-meaning people who want to understand what all the fuss is about. I propose that we stop fixating on the next awful thing the anti-abortion forces think up, and use our energy for a more proactive agenda. I hope you count yourself among the 37 percent of all women who has had an abortion or the 85 percent of partners who have been involved in an abortion decision, or the friend of someone who confided in you and shared her abortion story, or even one of the lucky parents who actually got to be involved in your daughter's pregnancy decision.[5] If so, you are fortunate enough to experience one of life's most eye-opening moments—and you *know*: You know that there are no easy answers. You know that choosing abortion doesn't mean wanting an abortion. You know that a woman's decision considers issues such as it not being the right time to have a child, or a partner not being the right person to be a parent to your child, or not having the right circumstances to bring a child into the world. To get that kind of profound insight into life may be hard, but it does bestow a kind of rare wisdom.

The general public may believe that women who have abortions are turning their backs on "life," as though the only life involved is that of the potential baby. In my experience as an abortion provider, I know that, really, they are turning toward life in the most responsible way they know how. The decision to end a pregnancy invariably means valuing the living, whether by choosing to care for an existing child or another person in need, or to focus on one's own future. This decision nearly always considers the quality of life a woman can offer a new life. If you have been privy to an abortion experience, you know the incredible complexity of such decisions Stop a minute to consider—as most pregnant women must—the intricate web of your life and what a new strand might do to the whole. Not everyone can experience this profound insight, but a pregnancy decision, no matter what is decided, is one way to do it.

I have one question for those of you who have had the opportunity to consider the complexity and weight of pregnancy. Why aren't you talking about it? Why wait to tell your daughter about your abortion experience until *after* she gets pregnant? Why don't you guys tell your new girlfriend what you learned about yourself when your ex-lover had an abortion? Or, better yet, why don't you tell your best friend? Why not talk about your own abortion? Have you considered revealing your personal experiences to others so that they might be comforted by and enlightened about what a shared experience this is?

I know why the answers to these questions are so often "no": *stigma*. Of course, no one wants others to think less of them or to question their motives or essential goodness. But really, this is profound stuff. Remember after 9/11 when burly cops cried at the drop of hat, and soccer moms couldn't drop off their kids without saying, "I love you," and everyone suddenly got cell phones so that they could "be there" no matter what happened? America was wandering around in a big, mushy emotional state until we went to war and shifted our emotions to the negative ones of collective fear and the focus on killing suspected terrorists. It was a national brush with death, and in that brief flash of light we got to see what was important to us. Sometimes a crisis of such magnitude can open our eyes and change our lives.

Likewise, an abortion experience can help clarify what is important to us personally: *I need to be there for the two kids I already have. I never realized how important going to school was going to be for me. What am I doing with this jerk? I do want a baby someday, but I want to be really ready.* There are 1.2 million potentially varied considerations and decisions (if all abortion experiences acknowledged this transformative power) that are made every year. More, if you count the partners, parents, and friends who have shared this experience.

In the unlikely event that you have never been part of this "in" crowd, where's your place in all of this? Your place is in acknowledging that this is complex stuff. Don't say, "*I* would decide to . . . " or "*I* would never . . . " You don't know what you would do, and you can't know until you're there. Try to appreciate what would happen if your life turned on the pink line of that pregnancy test. What hopes and fears would it raise for you? Ask someone what their experience has been. Ask your partner. Ask your parents. Ask your friends. And then listen. You still won't know what you would do in that situation, but you can get a feel for the texture of the decision-making. You might begin to feel the weight of the variables that go into a woman's individual decision and the feelings that come about when one path feels "right."

Try saying out loud—at work, school, or with your friends—"I have no idea what I would do if I/my partner were pregnant and didn't want to be, but I sure would want someone to talk to who wouldn't judge me."[6] Wait a week or two, and then don't be surprised if someone tells you their story. It might be a story about an unexpected pregnancy, a miscarriage, or something that made the person feel "not normal." There is no safety in the world for people to tell their abortion stories unless we make it safe. Remember, voice *out loud* your willingness to listen without judgment in a roomful of people.

It may take a little courage, in some cases tremendous courage. Breaking silence always does, and there may be a few murmurings that such conversation is not polite, or even some loudmouths who spew their hatred or ignorance at you. Good. It's important for everyone to know who they are and what they stand for. Reveal the bully, let him or her stand in their own narrow-mindedness. This is important work. The true value is in making room for those who have had an abortion experience to shed the stigma: *Maybe not everyone would think less of me.* Wouldn't this be profound?

Here's another thing that we have some power over: the post-abortion emotional health of women we know. Note the term: *post-abortion emotional health.* The antis say abortion is traumatic and results in "post-abortion stress syndrome (PASS)" and we have largely been mute about it until recently. There is a community of providers, researchers, clergy, social service workers, and others who care about women who are beginning to understand how they can get through a difficult pregnancy decision and actually come out emotionally healthier, if possible. We do not want to ignore that some women have a very hard time coping, and we want to be able to spot those at greatest risk for poor outcomes and help them.

The research evidence has not been as reassuring as we might want. "Most women feel relief after an abortion," say most pro-choice activists. This is true, but it is not the whole picture. Women are certainly capable of feeling more than one thing, and that mix of normal feelings may include sadness, guilt, anger, regret, and maybe even shame.[7] Go back to what you know from experience: No one wants to be pregnant when she didn't intend to be. It can certainly bring up a lot of "life" issues and feelings. Furthermore, because of the stigma, women may not feel comfortable confiding in people they normally talk to, and this silence may be a recipe for mental health trouble.

But traumatic? According to reliable research study (longitudinal, good sample size, peer reviewed, replicable, published studies by credentialed social scientists), 1 percent of women will have a traumatic reaction to abortion. That's a small percentage, but it still amounts to a large number, given that 1.2 million women have an abortion in a given year. But we should also place this statistic into a larger context. The rate of trauma reactions in the general population, for any reason, is 10.75 percent, and 46 percent of that 10.75 percent, as a result of sexual abuse and 48.5 percent as a result of childhood abuse.[8]

When we set the statistics aside and look at actual abortion experiences, we find that, for some women, the pregnancy crisis, or even having a medical procedure, can trigger an existing trauma. Others may react traumatically to such a major decision, or the experience itself, especially if they were previously against abortion. Other women have had a break in a relationship, either with a significant other or a parent. A few women feel so alone or have so few coping skills that they wind up suffering emotionally. And do we really know what the effect of societal condemnation and cultural silence is on a woman in the middle of an abortion experience? We don't need researchers to tell us it isn't good, but remember, 47 percent of women felt that if they told someone about their abortion, the person would think less of them. We also know that suppressing emotions and concealing important experiences can be harmful.

Many abortion providers are beginning to figure out which women are at the highest risk for poor emotional outcomes after their abortions and are thus able to offer some help and resources.[9] But there are still too many clinics where providers will not intervene, even if they see an emotional train wreck in the making. There's potential to create the most supportive abortion clinic in the country, but the question remains: What exists outside the clinic walls? The same picketers, stigmatizing cultural messages, and silence about the true complexity of an abortion decision, that's what.

Once again, it comes back to us—those closest to a woman or to a couple going through an abortion. Parents. Family. Partners. Best friends. Parents are often the least likely to be told, but the most likely, in the end, to provide help and comfort to their daughters or sons. It can be a bumpy road, especially for parents of adolescents who opt for abortion. Parents often say: "If you get pregnant, you'll be out on the street," and even though kids don't seem to listen to anything their parents have to say, this threat gets through loud and clear. Teenagers often say, "I can't tell my parents, they would be so *disappointed*." Many say, "My parents would kill me," and for some, it's not just a figure of speech. We have to ask ourselves why is it so rare for a parent to say, "I will always be there for you no matter what." Pro-choice people could do a lot more to promote communication between parents and their children on this subject, or at the very least, help prevent the most egregious mistakes a parent is likely to make in a moment of shock."[10] If we are going to be against parental consent and notification, we need to be *for* parental involvement so that young people have the most support possible. Laws need to take into account those who are the most vulnerable—kids with absent parents, kids in abusive homes, etc. At the same time, we can invite the involvement of parents who, while not happy, nevertheless support their children.

Who else are we abandoning? Those who rely on government insurance like Medicaid are on their own when it comes to paying for an abortion in most states.[11] So, what would you do if you could not pay for an abortion? Just like in the days when it was illegal, you might borrow ten or twenty dollars from a number of different people. You would put off paying your rent or utilities. You might pawn something. You might even beg. This kind of begging is not as visible as the street people in big cities, but our cultural responses are similar: Look the other way. (The "system" should do something.) Think it's their fault. (Why weren't they using birth control?) Give a little something but tell them not to spend it on drugs or booze. (No repeat abortions!) Americans are very judgmental when it comes to their money; it is widely understood in politics that a majority favors the right to an abortion, but access to it is not assured. If you can't afford your own healthcare, you are in for some moralizing about your behavior.

If you really want to understand the reality of abortion, volunteer for (and contribute to) one of the more than one hundred abortion funds that have sprouted up to help women get access to abortion services.[12] We can donate millions to rant about universal healthcare or try to reinstate Medicaid funding for abortions—good causes—but we can also choose to make the world more just and fair by putting money directly into women's hands to pay for essential reproductive services.

"But why didn't she use birth control?" If I had a dollar for every time that question has been asked, we wouldn't need abortion funding. Here's a secret: Birth control is not as effective as we want it to be. The public is lulled into thinking that condoms, for instance, are 90 percent effective, or that the Pill is 99 percent effective. All abortion providers know that the methods themselves are fallible and that "perfect use" is only theoretical. More importantly, why do we demand perfection of others and ignore our own risk-taking? Truth time: We all take risks when it comes to sex. I would argue that it is probably hardwired into our genes. It's Mother Nature's relentless agenda to get us pregnant every month, so that otherwise perfectly responsible, sensible people end up throwing themselves at each other—birth control be damned.

If you cannot relate to risk-taking around sex, how about speeding in your car? How about the thrill-seeking of contact sports? How about overeating or drinking too much? Taking risks is human nature, and although we usually avoid serious damage, the consequences can be grave. So inventory your own life, especially your youthful indiscretions, and lighten up on the judgment. Go further: Acknowledge that sex is a normal part of life. There is some research that suggests that if we start from a position of accepting our sexual selves as adolescents and as adults, we are better able to protect ourselves from the risks inherent in sexual encounters (emotional risks, as well as pregnancy, HIV, STI, etc.).[13] Our unintended-pregnancy rates are among the highest in the industrialized world and our inability to talk realistically about sex and birth control surely contributes to our embarrassing world ranking.

Earlier I suggested that an abortion experience is "fortunate" because of the wisdom it can impart. This is an intentional reframing of a personal crisis to illuminate the possible enlightenment that can result from a pregnancy decision. There is another unspoken potential that could come from an abortion experience—fetal-tissue research. American scientists have been disadvantaged by our government's reactionary response to stem-cell research. While most of the attention in this country has been focused on stem cells from extra embryos from fertility treatments, other countries are making valuable use of embryonic and fetal material obtained from abortions, with the enthusiastic consent of the women donors.

Imagine, then, that a woman (you or someone you know) becomes pregnant and for whatever reasons cannot continue the pregnancy. She chooses abortion reluctantly because she knows the stigma against those who choose to end a pregnancy. At the clinic, she is treated compassionately and offered the opportunity to donate her pregnancy tissue to help others. In the midst of a complicated stew of personal upheaval and societal censure, suddenly she thinks, "Something good can come out of this." And it can, because around the world, fetal tissue is being used to treat heart problems, severe burns, diabetes, and a host of other diseases. In all places where tissue donation is an option, there is no economic profit for individual women, doctors, clinics, or researchers, and through the generosity of these individuals, a life event that might otherwise be seen as a tragedy, a sin, or a piece of bad luck can be transformed into one of the most life-affirming acts a woman could offer the world.

Can we imagine a world where each of us, through our everyday actions, changes a negative into a positive? A world where women who feel that everyone will think less of them because of their abortion instead are honored for the wisdom and compassion their experience imparts? Can we create such a world through our own ability to listen and speak out? Can we acknowledge that while abortion cuts off one potential, it also opens up many more opportunities for life?

Yes, we can. And each of us can say it in our own way, out loud, to as many people as possible.

THE RHETORIC OF ABORTION
Reflections from a Former Pro-Life Activist
ELIZABETH WARDLE, PhD

In the house and church I grew up in, there was no question about where I would stand on abortion.

A fetus was a life.

We opposed taking life.

Case closed.

What conversation can be had when only one question is considered pertinent? I was a chaste, Christian, small-town, pro-life teenager from a happy home with two parents. My most exciting experiences were church camping trips. At sixteen, I had never even kissed a boy. Nothing had ever happened to me to suggest other questions were relevant in the abortion debate. I was sure of my views and sure my experiences provided enough information with which to make an informed decision about what was right for all women everywhere. Thus, I goaded my girlfriends into attending protests and meetings and starting teenage pro-life groups. No one questioned me. Where we came from, my girlfriends were wrong not to have thought of going to the meetings before I did. They admired my staunch, unquestioning sense of what was right and wrong. Looking back, it's clear I was pompous, self-righteous, and unbearably certain of myself. But I had the total peace of mind that only comes from a worldview with no shades of gray.

My certainty and peace of mind were not to last, however. College showed me that life is full of gray.

In college I discovered that some people have sex without feeling they have done something dirty, that women get pregnant who are in no position to take care of a child, and that one of the most frightening things in the world for an eighteen-year-old from a pro-life, Christian fundamentalist family would be telling her parents she was pregnant. If I had become pregnant and informed my parents, I knew exactly where I would have gone: straight to a home for pregnant teenage mothers, to be physically well-cared for and proselytized to for nine months, after which time my child would have been adopted by a good, white fundamentalist family dying for a healthy new (white) baby. I would have been shamed. My parents' biggest concern would have been how to hide my pregnancy from their friends. Problematic as this response would have been, it pales in comparison to what has actually happened to other Christian teenagers who have been disowned, thrown out of their homes, and even physically harmed. It later came as no surprise that, according to the Alan Guttmacher Institute, one in five women seeking abortions is a born-again or an Evangelical Christian. Had I become pregnant as a teenager, I would have done all in my power—including consider an abortion—to avoid the shame I would have felt in the eyes of my Christian community.

I began to understand why parental-consent laws might be a bad idea: They can raise the number of late-term abortions, because young women from conservative homes may put off a decision or wait for parental or judicial consent. Some pregnant teens would even choose illegal abortions rather than face their parents' wrath.

In my women's studies classes I learned about poverty and racism, about misogyny, about the history of birth control (or rather, control of birth control). I learned that for many women, there are several important questions that come before the one that asks whether or not a fetus is a life—questions such as, "Will this pregnancy cost me my life? Who will feed this child? Where is one person who will provide me with some support if I have this child?" I learned that two out of three women who have abortions say they cannot afford a child, and half do not have a dependable partner with earning potential. In one study, Glen Stassen, the Lewis B. Smedes Professor of Christian Ethics at Fuller Theological Seminary, found a clear correlation between unemployment rates, healthcare costs, and abortion rates.[1]

The more I learned, the more I began to let go of my carefully held certainties.

After my worldview took on a few more shades of gray, my friends started telling me about their abortions. I had to come to terms with the fact that the women against whom I had so emphatically protested in high school were good people, people I knew, people I would want for my friends. What to do with that? Love the sinner, hate the sin? Fairly easy to say in Christian theory, but my friends didn't seem like sinners. They seemed like girls who had fallen in love, or been taken advantage of, or even raped.

I started to wonder about sin, and why so much sin in the Christian tradition falls on women and centers around women's bodies.

By the end of college, my former certainty about abortion had completely deserted me. I had arrived at a place where I couldn't identify myself as pro-life any longer. I now believed in choice, but without advocating abortion. I still believed a fetus was a life—but I had come to understand there were other issues at stake, too. Was mine a pro-choice position? None of the pro-choice rhetoric with which I was familiar led me to believe it was; having once been a true believer in the pro-life movement, I found nothing in the rhetoric of the pro-choice movement that appealed to me or adequately stated my position.

Those against choice gained the upper hand in the rhetorical battle over abortion long ago. They won a major victory when they managed to convince even their foes to refer to them by the rhetorically persuasive term "pro-life." (After all, who isn't for life?) Pro-lifers have the much stronger rhetorical position, both verbally and visually. They believe they have God on their side, and they convincingly convey the righteousness of their position in every statement they make. They compare abortion to the Holocaust—a metaphor no one for choice can rival. They have pictures of what they claim are aborted fetuses, fetuses that appear both human and violently damaged. Such pictures appeal to pathos in a way no logical pro-choice argument can hope to.

Members of the pro-choice movement are not entirely to blame for their inability to match the rhetorical strength of their opponents. Second-wave feminists who fought for legalized abortion witnessed or experienced illegal abortions and all the terror caused by them; they translated this horror into the moving symbol of a coat hanger. However, that symbol is rhetorically empty for women of my generation forward. As a result, the pro-choice movement simply does not have competing images for those placed on placards by the anti-choice movement. As long as abortion is legal and safe, there is (thankfully) no image to rival the visual horror of an aborted fetus; instead, there are only sterile, unemotional concepts in which to believe: privacy, choice, legalization. While feminists may feel the rightness of choice, that rightness can't compare, on an emotional level, to the emotions associated with the implied opposite of pro-life (pro-death) or with the images of bloody fetuses.

But part of the loss of the rhetorical war *is* the fault of pro-choice feminists; for decades they have reacted to the terms set by anti-choice conservatives, simultaneously alienating women like me, who are for choice but not for abortion. I'd like to see us engage in a new discussion, employing new terms, contexts, and standards; being proactive instead of reactive.

Here is a pro-choice position I can get behind:

Abortion is generally not the problem in need of our attention. In most cases, abortion is one result of a number of related problems; abortion is wrapped up in intimate ways with attitudes about sex, living wages, access to good jobs, healthcare, childcare, education, and so on.

If we want to prevent bringing unwanted or unsupported life into this world, birth control must be accessible to all; men and women alike need education about the necessities of birth control.

Birth control, sex education, and factually correct abstinence-only programs are abortion issues.

Girls from conservative homes like mine do not need lectures about the shame of sex, but about the beauties and dangers of sex, and ways to avoid the dangers. They must learn to love their bodies, draw appropriate boundaries, and know what precautions to take when they are ready for sex.

Hatred of women and women's bodies in the Christian tradition are abortion issues.

Women from all walks of life must make a living wage so they can support children when they are ready to have them. If two-thirds of all women who seek abortions say they cannot afford a child, improving economic conditions by providing viable job opportunities for both men and women should greatly decrease the number of abortions.[2]

Raising the minimum wage is an abortion issue.

Women everywhere must have affordable healthcare for themselves and their children, so they can bring healthy children into the world and keep them healthy.[3]

Affordable universal healthcare is an abortion issue.

Women must have access to quality daycare that will not cost more than they make at work.

Government-subsidized child care is an abortion issue.

Women must have access to affordable education so they can compete for living-wage jobs, and so they can promise that same access to their children.

Education-related government grants and loans are abortion issues.

Adoption must be demystified, shown to be a loving and generous choice, not abandonment.

Adoption laws, adoption agency regulations and oversight, and attitudes about adoption are abortion issues.

To engage in productive dialogue about abortion, we must account for justice and equity; we must strive to make our country one where laws, practices, programs, and attitudes nurture women and allow them the opportunity to bring babies into the world when they can support them, provide them excellent healthcare, send them to college without putting themselves in massive debt, and promise them truthfully that there are living-wage jobs waiting for them.

Come to think of it, if this isn't a genuinely pro-life position, I don't know what is.

HOW TO TALK (REALLY TALK) ABOUT ABORTION

CAROLINA DE ROBERTIS

ALTHOUGH A MILLION WOMEN AND MEN FLOODED WASHINGTON,
D.C., for the 2004 March for Women's Lives, very few made eye contact
with me once they read my T-shirt: I HAD AN ABORTION. Their eyes met
my chest but could not make their way to the face of the woman who
bore the message. Their glances shifted away, and onto the next placard.
Two young women took a moment from chanting to hug me and tell me
I was brave. A woman from "the other side" approached me with a face
drenched in compassion, and handed me an informational card. "I Regret My Abortion," it read. "If you do too, there's help."

Amid streams of pro-choice people, I felt something of a leper.
At the end of the day, I ran into an acquaintance, a friend of a friend,
toting a dozen placards. She volunteered for the Feminist Majority
Foundation, and was gathering the signs that now lay strewn across

the grass. I knew that she'd devoted the past three weeks to tireless work on behalf of the march. She looked exhausted, but thrilled. Her eyes shone.

"Wasn't it *amazing?*" she exclaimed. She began talking, a mile a minute, about the victories of the day: the incredible turnout, the rousing speeches, the powerful message sent to anti-choice legislators.

As we continued to talk, I slipped out of my cardigan.

"Oh," she said, "What does your shirt say?"

I watched as her previously animated expression turned to shock. She looked at me with a mixture of embarrassment and horror. Finally she said, "I'm sorry."

"Thanks," I replied, a bit alarmed at her gravity. I almost added, *I'm not sorry.* But whether or not I was sorry wasn't the issue (too often, "sorry" and "not sorry" boxes women's stories into "right" and "wrong" camps). So I kept silent.

She quickly changed the subject, launching into a tirade against politicians who are trying to take our reproductive rights away. She was enraged, almost shouting. Though her anger wasn't directed at me, it felt as though my disclosure had somehow sparked it.

This was not the first time I had been so outwardly open about having had an abortion. As a co-founder of Exhale, the nation's first and only after-abortion talkline (phone counseling service) that respects reproductive freedom, I had spoken about my abortion experience many times before to trainees and audiences as well as friends and family. Even so, it felt jarring to be met with horror, embarrassment, and then a general rage. I wondered how another woman, one who had never disclosed her abortion before, might have felt in this situation. I imagined that it would not have been easy.

This experience reminded me of a story I'd heard of a pro-choice woman who'd stopped going to marches after her abortion. All those chants and slogans brought her feelings to the surface, and she feared those feelings would not be welcomed by pro-choice activists. In that moment, standing in the ebbing crowd, I was able to empathize with her. In the weeks that followed the March for Women's Lives, I thought more about the woman with the placards. I was struck by her reaction to my T-shirt—her gut sense that my abortion must have been something horrible—and I remembered how she'd mentioned that she had been raised Baptist. She had said this in a manner that suggested her current political beliefs stood in stark contrast to her religious background. There she was, a woman of color, working with a primarily white, pro-choice organization. What opportunities, I wondered, had she had to freely discuss her values—whether cultural or personal—about abortion? Did she ever feel pressured, in her work for abortion rights, to fit into a box of beliefs that didn't completely fit her? The rhetoric of the mainstream pro-choice movement proscribes that most women feel relief after an abortion, and that those who don't (or feel relief plus something else) are an unfortunate minority, suffering from other problems, ranging from poverty to histories of depression or abuse.

The pro-choice mainstream has its taboo subjects, such as questions about the nature of the fetus. Though the current rhetoric evolved as a political strategy for defending abortion rights, its narrow language can also be a detriment to women's rights because it ultimately alienates people who want to support legal abortion but have beliefs, experiences, and values that don't fit this simplistic framework. Because the pro-choice rhetoric is largely shaped by white leaders, and therefore white culture, it often translates into a negation of the perspectives of communities of color.

It is still charged and risky to talk about abortion publicly—the act of abortion itself—and how it affects people's everyday lives. Abortion is a subject under siege. There are two embattled fronts, and each side has laid claim to limited language that defends its position.

Meanwhile, women are having abortions: one in three women in the United States will have one in her lifetime. If you know more than three women, you're closer to abortion than you might realize. All of us, collectively, set the tone of the social climate, which determines whether those who've had abortions encounter shame and judgments or whether they encounter respect and support. All of us possess the power to engage in open conversation or turn away from it. But I believe women's health and rights strengthen when we talk—*really talk*—about abortion.

My earliest memory of a frank discussion about abortion was at age twelve, when a group of my friends pondered the question, "Would you rather be raped or have an abortion, if you had to choose?"

We were the perfect age for weighing morbid options against each other—like dying in a fire versus falling off a cliff. My friends all chose abortion; I chose rape.

I was too young to know that my hypothetical decision was politically unacceptable to roughly half the country, and political fodder for roughly the other half who oppose abortion. I just knew that, when I thought of ever having an abortion, I felt a terrible sadness, and a sense of tragedy. It didn't seem like murder; it seemed like the surrender of something precious, like being forced by circumstance to give away a trove of treasure.

The difference between my friends and me may have in part been cultural. I spent my teenage years in a white, middle-class neighborhood in Los Angeles. Though I shared economic status and skin color with my white friends, inside my family's house was an Uruguayan world, in which having children was assumed to be the pinnacle of my future and tampons were reserved for married women. My values about pregnancy were shaped by my Latina culture, but they were also intimately my own. I had a relationship to my womb that was deeply personal. No one told me to linger on the toilet during my first year of menstruation so that, in awe, I could watch my blood drip. That was a secret all mine, a piece of my private truth.

I started having sex when I was seventeen. In a stroke of good fortune, I had a wonderful and healthy first experience with sex. My boyfriend was kind and eager, a virgin himself. I told him that if he ever entered me without protection, or even thought about it, I'd never speak to him again. We kept speaking. Six months in, I decided to get a diaphragm.

Then, at eighteen, during my first year of college, I got pregnant.

I was horrified. I'd been vigilant to the point of being paranoid. *How could this happen to me?* It didn't take me long to figure out that the gynecologist who'd prescribed the diaphragm had neglected to inform me that diaphragms don't work as well without spermicide. Later, when I confronted him, he blamed the "misunderstanding" on my age and ignorance.

But none of this made me any less pregnant. Abortion was—to me then, now, and every day since—the best decision I could have made. I'd just started college; I lived with my parents; I was completely financially dependent. I wanted children desperately, but I couldn't imagine supporting them when I still hadn't figured out how to support myself.

My pregnancy was unplanned, but it was not unwanted. It was deeply wanted, with gut and heart and womb and soul. But there was friction between what I wanted and the real world around me—with the economic pressures, lack of widespread childcare, and penalization of motherhood in schools and in the workplace.

My pregnancy pushed me up against the core of my spiritual beliefs. I reflected fiercely on life, death, and whatever lay beyond. I spoke to the spirit that was not going to be born (or, at least, not with me). I named her and told her that I loved her and always would. I tried very hard not to love being pregnant. I also tried to avoid the mangled baby photos strewn across the UCLA campus by pro-life students.

On the day of my abortion, the doctor didn't look me in the eye or even speak to me. She went about her business, and afterward the counselor foisted birth control pills on me. I still wasn't sure how I felt about hormonal methods, but I didn't resist: I was medicated and, well, had just had an abortion. And besides, it appeared that I could no longer be trusted to know what I wanted. The clinician's demeanor suggested that I was incapable of determining which birth control method was right for me. Based on the sheer fact that I'd ended up on their table, I was made to feel that birth control choices were a conferred privilege, like a driver's license, and I'd just had the reproductive equivalent of a car crash. I accepted the pills and went home.

In the weeks after my abortion, I lactated. I'd only been pregnant for six weeks, and had no idea such a thing could happen. When the milk was finally gone, I remember turning in bed, in the dark, to face the wall. It was one of the saddest moments of my life.

In the years that followed, I never regretted my decision. I did, however, experience waves of grief, sadness, love, and rage. My life was not the same. I began to speak with women about my experience, and was surprised to hear the range of stories that emerged. One friend of mine had had three abortions, and kept a potted plant for each one of them in her home. Another friend did a series of paintings of herself with an infant who grew steadily older. The mother of another friend told me that when her son was born she recognized him as the spirit of the baby she'd aborted years before. This gave her a sense of peace with her experience that she hadn't had before. Yet another friend felt no particular connection with the fetus, and barely thought about her abortion afterward. No story was more valid than another.

I was fortunate to exchange stories with these women—to feel their support and learn of processes for closure and release. But I still wish that over the years there had been a safe, anonymous place to express feelings about my abortion as they arose. I wish this for all of us.

I met Aspen Baker in 2000. She volunteered at the rape crisis center where I worked and she wanted to start a "talkline" for women who'd had abortions. My first thought was, *Wild horses cannot keep me from this project.*

By that time, I was fueled by both professional and personal experience. As a rape crisis counselor, I'd had some clients who'd had abortions after pregnancies caused by rape. I recognized the lack of resources for these women. Nothing existed that could meet the emotional needs of women who were opting to have abortions that didn't entail funneling them through a political agenda. What these women felt varied widely: Some were glad they'd had an abortion and needed to hear it was okay to feel that way; others were grieving deeply, convinced they'd never be forgiven for the sin of killing their baby.

I had one client who has never left my mind. On the day of her abortion, she told her providers that the pregnancy was the result of rape. The providers had to call the police, in compliance with the law. The date happened to coincide with the six-year anniversary of my own abortion. I held her hand through the police report, the abortion procedure, then the rest of the police report. She came to visit me once a week for some months afterward. She spoke no English and her whole family was in Mexico. She was a devout Catholic, and had never had consensual sex. She believed she'd never be forgiven for the terrible sin of abortion. Healing from rape, for her, meant expressing great pain about her abortion, and the ways it intertwined with her immigration experience, economic barriers, linguistic stigma, isolation, racism, religion, and her very personal relationship with God. Outside our counseling room, she had nowhere to talk about it. My memory of her was part of what fueled me on the road of co-creating Exhale.

The five co-founders—all women in our twenties and thirties and from a range of personal and professional backgrounds—began meeting that summer. We were women who'd had abortions and women who'd helped friends through abortions. We all saw the need for safe places to talk about personal experiences with abortion.

For a year and a half, we met regularly in each other's living rooms. We researched service models, raised funds through our networks, and, most importantly, articulated our common vision for Exhale. What did it mean to provide a nonjudgmental counseling phone service on such a politicized topic? What are the after-abortion emotional needs of women, and how could we meet them? What tools and approaches would be necessary to make our service accessible to every woman? And what about men?

We dove into these questions, grappling with their many intricacies. We were vulnerable about our own stories and our beliefs about what pregnancy and the fetus really meant to us. We examined the language and labels of the political debate and asked ourselves how our service could use language in a manner that meets women where they are. We developed a model designed to respect and support each individual's unique experience, regardless of what their feelings or beliefs about abortion might be. We drew tools from other contexts, such as rape crisis counseling models, that could meet our callers where they were without imposing our own judgments. We agreed that our service would respect reproductive freedom, but we would refrain from using political labels that might limit our accessibility to some callers. We were neither pro-choice nor pro-life; we were something more encompassing than those terms, something that affirmed the voice of each woman who'd had an abortion. A few years later, we named our approach "pro-voice."

In the fall of 2001, we trained our first group of counselors. In January of 2002, our talkline opened as a local, all-volunteer service in the San Francisco Bay Area. We received our first call on our second night of operation. In the first year, we received 308 calls and were overwhelmed with requests for resources and information from all over the country. From 2002 to 2004, our call volume increased, we created new programs to meet the national demand for training and public education, and our paid staff grew from zero to a whopping two. In June 2005, in response to increased demand, we became accessible nationwide, in four languages. Our call volume rose 400 percent in the first month.

Each call to the talkline, like each caller, is as unique as a fingerprint. There is no way to generalize what callers are looking for—except that they are looking for a place to talk about their experience with abortion. Some want to talk about their feelings—grief, relief, isolation, frustration with unsupportive partners or friends, guilt about overburdening supportive partners or friends, pride, shame, sadness, loss, empowerment, regret, confusion, and the unexpected mix of feelings they are experiencing. Some call us with concrete concerns, such as how to comfort a family member; whether or not to disclose their abortion to friends or family; how to make peace with God; how to cope with seeing infants in public; how to create closure with the fetus or spirit or baby or thing; how to take time out for themselves.

We do not tell people what to do. Saying there is a "right" way to respond after an abortion is like saying there is one "right" experience, or one "right" culture. Each caller is her or his own best expert on the context and realities of their life. Instead, we support each caller in exploring their options, and in finding an approach that is best for them.

The approaches our callers have found to define their experience are a testament to their strength and resourcefulness, and to the dazzling range of personal experience with abortion.

Talking about abortion does not have to be confined to a talkline. It can happen anywhere: at our dinner tables, at rallies, at the water cooler, in classrooms and community groups, with family and friends. We can talk with those who agree with us and those who don't; we can even move beyond the stilted discourse of with-me-or-against-me and listen to the depth of thoughts from people across the spectrum. This can be a powerful act, but it must occur in a climate of mutual respect.

Creating such a climate means valuing each woman who has had an abortion enough to validate her experience, even if her perspective differs from our own. It means exploring the nitty-gritty of our own beliefs, and giving others room to do the same. It means challenging our own embedded cultural assumptions, prejudices, and knee-jerk judgments (we've all got them). It means placing value on women and their voices. In short: It means becoming pro-voice.

In doing so, we can further each woman's right to control her body, *and* express her truth, *and* seek the things that make her healthy, strong, and whole.

THE POLITICAL IS PERSONAL, or GOD BLESS AMERICA

ALANA BIBEAU

THE PROCESS OF COMING TO KNOW THAT I WAS PREGNANT SEEMED long and drawn out, like when you wait for summer to arrive and then all at once, and without warning, you are in the thick of it. I was optimistically impatient, looking for the familiar comfort of that monthly blood swirling in the toilet bowl, cursing the swelling breasts while simultaneously explaining away their unusual tenderness and trying to ignore the pinching sensation in my lower abdomen. They were just reassurances that my period, though meandering a bit, was on its way.

I discovered my predicament in the bathroom of a fast-food restaurant. It was a week before my twenty-fifth birthday and a month before my boyfriend and I were to pack up and move six hundred miles away to a state we'd visited only once so that I could begin my

PhD in sociology. The drugstore where we purchased the test was next to the fast-food restaurant where my father treated himself to a bacon cheeseburger every day on his lunch break from a job he hated. Since I was so confident that I was just being overly cautious, I persuaded my boyfriend to hop into hamburger hell so I could relieve us both of the burden of worry that had begun to creep into our bones. I figured it would only take a minute and then we would hop back out into the night, off to whichever watering hole or rock-and-roll show or friend's house we had been headed.

Not quite. We ended up driving to a parking lot outside the city, where we sat for two hours and talked ourselves inside out. I had already made the decision to terminate the pregnancy the moment I saw those two pink lines on that twelve-dollar wand, but it warranted dialogue nonetheless. What I didn't know at the time was that what seemed like a black-and-white decision politically, and even personally when I was making it, would come to feel more ambiguous as time went on.

I had been raised Catholic in a working-class suburb of Providence, Rhode Island. Both my parents, my sister, and most of my relatives and family friends, as far as I could tell, would identify as pro-life, if pressed. I was the black sheep, the freak, the weirdo, the hippie, the radical, the *feminist* in my family. I had been conscious of my position from an early age, though not always. Somewhere between seeing pictures of aborted fetuses on pamphlets at the church we attended when I was in elementary school and volunteering as an escort at the Planned Parenthood downtown when I was in college, my politics had emerged, full-force. By the time I started college, I knew that I would double-major in women's studies and sociology; the notion that women, not the government—or the church—should have control over their own bodies seemed glaringly apparent, and access to safe, legal abortion came with the territory.

My boyfriend had been raised in a different neighborhood in the same suburban city by his old-school, hippieish parents. Though his mother stayed home to raise him and his two younger brothers while his father worked, they had lived together before getting married and their politics seemed—compared to my church-choir-singing parents—fairly liberal. Despite the fact that religion had not been a part of his upbringing, we were pretty confident his parents would not have been thrilled with the idea of their unmarried son and his girlfriend becoming parents ("So soon?" I could hear his mother asking in her sweet way, trying not to judge but failing miserably), or with the idea that I was deciding to terminate their first potential grandchild. They were having a hard enough time dealing with our move south.

And so we decided to keep it to ourselves, but still to go through it together. But going through it together, as only someone who has had an abortion can know, really means going it alone. The first thing I did was name the sack of tissue growing inside of me. I called it "America." This way, I figured, when I thought back on the pro-lifers who would greet me at the clinic entrance and tell me how selfish I was being, how God would take care of me and my child, I could think to myself, *God Bless America.* When I called the clinic, they told me the only date they had available for me to come in was two days before my birthday. Since it was early enough in the pregnancy, I had decided to have what's called a medical abortion, rather than a surgical one. This meant that I would have the abortion at home, after taking two pills that day at the clinic and inserting a third into my vagina—at home, on the day I should have celebrated turning twenty-five. Throughout the day, after calling the clinic, I secretly hummed "God Bless America," the song which had quickly become my anthem. Maybe not the day I would have chosen if I had a choice, I reminded myself, but *at least I have a choice.*

At the last minute, I decided to tell my mother. I sat her down and informed her that I was going to be sick on my birthday, in and out of the bathroom. She just looked at me, with kindness in her eyes, and said, "You're pregnant, aren't you?" without a hint of judgment. I asked her not to tell my father and she never did. It was only then, in that moment, that I understood the unconditional love that parents must have for their children—*should* have, need to *learn* to have—and I was comforted. And we cried together, and laughed through our tears, whispering, "God Bless America."

On the day my boyfriend and I drove to the clinic, I was calm and clear, like a pond or a lake just before you heave a flat, heavy stone into it. We stopped for frozen lemonades on the way. It was hot, as it always is that time of year. July. The week of my birthday. The whole time in the car and in the waiting room I was so sedate compared to what I would have expected. My memory of the clinic itself has become more impressionistic than literal, hiding in shadows in my mind. I remember the sound of the buzzer that let us into the building; the hair color of the nurse who took my blood was the same auburn shade as the Cabbage Patch Corn Silk Kid that belonged to my sister when she was six; the social worker's deep, dark tan, and her acrylic nails painted a shade of pink that I'm convinced only exists in certain parts of Rhode Island where 1980s fashion is still in vogue. And then there was the ultrasound machine.

The nurse practitioner had asked if I wanted to look at the screen. "Sometimes it helps," she said. I looked and I struggled to see life in the black and grayscale fuzz on the high tech screen. Maybe it was there. Maybe it wasn't. If I had decided to carry the fetus to term, the development of that potential life would have become of primary importance to me. But in the end, I lacked the emotional, financial, and social resources that would have made me feel good about bringing that life to fruition. The gravity of the situation, and of my decision, was never lost on me. But neither was the gravity of the situation for the millions of women and children living in poverty who lack the financial and social support they need. I did not want to become one of them.

A year after the abortion, my younger sister found out she was pregnant. She was engaged to be married at the time, but still living with my parents and employed as an overworked, underpaid case manager at a social service agency. When she came to me with the news, I offered her all the emotional support I knew how to give, along with the clinic's phone number, assuming that she would at least call them for information. I could not imagine bringing a child into the world in her position: no money, newly engaged, having never lived away from home. But she and her fiancé, mostly for religious reasons, opted to become parents, and I, in turn, became an aunt. One day, several months after my niece was born, I was flashing pictures and telling one of my friends another of my favorite baby stories, when she asked me, "Do you sometimes feel like she's your baby?"

I was there with my sister for the birth, and I love that child more than I've ever loved anyone or anything in the world. But I see how they struggle—mom and baby. Dad never home, always at work or out with friends. Gender division of household labor, and guess who gets the second shift (and if there's such a thing, the third and fourth)? Always trying to make ends meet, just so. My sister is a fabulous mother, and my niece is a happy, healthy little wonder. Sometimes I find myself feeling jealous. After all, we still live in a culture that values women as either sex objects or as mothers, and while there are clearly a range of options available to women today, society still rewards us, unmistakably, when we fit into one of these two extremes. Why doesn't anyone want to reward me for getting a PhD and choosing to forego motherhood, at least for the time being? Alternately, I find myself feeling grateful. What would it be like if I had carried the child to term? How would I ever manage with a child a year older than my niece is now?

I never would have managed. Or I would have managed poorly. Emotional and financial support are one thing, but without social support for mothering (which this country lacks), I would have had to compromise my education, my career, or my parenting in order to work at providing a good life for myself and my child.

When I moved away from New England and "down South" to start my doctoral work, it never occurred to me that I'd be facing a barrage of conservative, anti-woman academics, politicians, and activists. It was only recently, however, that I noticed that something about my own politics has changed, as well. Back in college and for years afterwards, when it came to pro-choice issues, I was always on the front lines, never afraid to confront someone in a debate. Now, when the pro-life Bible-thumpers show up on the campus where I work and study, I find myself not only *not* wanting to confront them, but wanting to run away from them. When I see a woman, younger than I am, with two kids under the age of three, her pregnant belly bulging, standing outside of the campus library with an oversized poster of an aborted fetus and wanting to debate me over abortion, I find myself wanting to cry. Not because I am ashamed or regretful of my decision, or because I am any less committed to pro-choice issues than I was before. No, it's because I think this woman and I are speaking different languages. She can put on a happy face and act like there's nothing at stake, because God will protect her and her children. But what about me? I feel like everything is at stake.

I think about the kind of parent I would have made at twenty-five and of the kind of aunt I make now. I think of the kind of parent I will make someday when, and if, I finally decide to have children. I think about the state of the world and I question whether this is the kind of place I even want to bring another child into. I think about wealthy, white academics and movie stars who travel to China, Russia, and South America to adopt their rainbow-colored families when there are thousands of poor, black children waiting to be adopted living within a sixty-mile radius of them. I sometimes wear my I HAD AN ABORTION T-shirt when I teach, not as a fashion statement or to brag about it, but because—to paraphrase what Audre Lorde so poignantly stated many years ago—my silence will not protect me. Everything is at stake. When I think about changes in the pro-choice movement, the ground we've lost over the last decade, and how high the stakes have become, about the tools that feminism has and has not given me in my struggle, it is this I know: The personal is political, for certain. But the political is also deeply, profoundly, personal.

BIRTH IS NOT ALWAYS BEST
Confessions of an Unwanted Child
DIANA HUET DE GUERVILLE

I HAVE NEVER HAD AN ABORTION, BUT I DO HAVE AN ABORTION story to share, from the perspective of a child only half-wanted.

This tale begins rather romantically, in the early 1970s, when a smart, young American woman travels to France to study political science, and falls in love with a Frenchman full of ambition and brimming with potential. After just four months together, they get married, move to the United States, and the new bride sacrifices her college studies to invest in her husband's engineering studies at the University of Michigan. In the United States, she works full-time as a secretary and moonlights as a ghostwriter for the foreign students who, like her husband, struggle with the English language. Before too long, she becomes pregnant. They are barely getting by, and abortion has only recently been legalized in the United States, but the twenty-one-year-old woman desperately wants this baby. On a long

November night, she gives birth to her first child. The new mother is so ecstatic that she decrees Joy as her daughter's middle name.

Meanwhile, the father feels unprepared for fatherhood given their dire economic situation and the demands of his American studies. He feels betrayed by his wife, who told him she was taking birth control and then insisted on having the baby. He is convinced that she became pregnant on purpose, that she forced him into having this child before he finished school, because she was "bored" and "impatient." The birth of this daughter has ruined all his plans for their future and has plunged them into poverty.

My mother wanted me; my father did not. Nor did he want the second child they would bring into the world three years later. I know this because they fought endlessly about the subject, especially when my brother or I needed something: a new pair of shoes, money for a field trip, even school supplies. "She tricked me!" my father would complain to us, full of resentment at the demands we placed on him, the lifestyle he couldn't attain because of our "constant chirping mouths." Over and over, he took on the wounded victim role, casting my mother as the irresponsible bully who forced him into fatherhood before he was ready, before he had the chance to live as an adult with a little freedom and some disposable income. My brother and I suffered the emotional abuse of hearing on a regular basis that we were unwanted and unwelcome, of being told that my father had a vasectomy after my brother was born so that my mother couldn't "trick him" into having any more children. Our very existence was fraught with tension. Regardless of how much my mother proclaimed her love for us, our father's resentment felt much stronger.

I first learned about abortion as a teenager, and began wondering if my parents had debated that option. I imagined an impassioned dialogue between their younger selves, with my father making rational arguments for terminating the pregnancy, and my mother making an emotional plea to have me. If they did have such an argument, she, as always, got her way. Yet I was convinced that she had made a mistake by dragging me into a world where I didn't belong. The first time I came across a bumper sticker reading EVERY CHILD A WANTED CHILD, I felt a shock of recognition in my tender teenage soul. *That should be the law of the universe,* I told myself, for I knew too well that being unwanted is devastating to the spirit. What is the point of being born for that?

Full of adolescent petulance, I became increasingly confrontational with my parents about the subject of my birth. In the midst of their fights, I screamed that I wished I had never been born, that they should've aborted me if my father hadn't wanted me. Though he was not cruel enough to concur, he did not disagree with me. My flustered mother insisted that she had wanted me enough for the both of them, but this only further enraged me. I despised my dad for vacillating between resentment and utter disinterest in me, but I blamed my mother for selfishly imposing my existence on a hostile man who felt burdened by my birth. In my deepest, wounded heart, I felt certain that abortion would have been the right choice for all of us.

Now that I'm past the volcanic agony of those teen years, on most days I'm glad to be alive. However, my story is not one of reverent gratitude for my mother's determination to keep me. The emotional abuse I suffered was significant and I will always bear those scars. Unlike those who oppose abortion from a sense of relief that their own lives were spared, my painful experience convinced me early on that it's not always in the best interest of the child to be born. I'm sure I would have become pro-choice no matter what; after all, my mother raised me to be an independent thinker, and I discovered feminism and progressive politics early on. However, knowing that one of my parents didn't want me (and told me so repeatedly), my politics regarding abortion were formed around the sense that abortion can be the most compassionate choice for the potential child.

Today, I work as a reproductive rights activist, and spend my days defending a woman's right to choose. The irony, which does not escape me, is that my mother did actually choose me. The problem, however, is that most of the language around choice is based on the woman as the primary decision-maker, and lost in this discourse is the role of the biological father. What happens when two potential parents want different outcomes? As a feminist, I believe that the woman must be the final decision-maker since she experiences the pregnancy, and she typically bears most, if not all, of the child-rearing responsibility. But then I remember my father's righteous rage at being forced to raise children he wasn't financially or emotionally ready for, and I worry about those born to men who are made to support children they would otherwise have chosen not to have.

At the other extreme, I have male friends who felt that they ultimately had no choice in their partner's decision to end her pregnancy, and grieved deeply for the loss of a child that they wanted. I have not always been patient with these friends, insisting that the woman must have the final choice, yet I do ask myself, *What, in a movement centered on women's rights, is the role of men? Where is there room for men's grief?* It seems to me that the personal is political for men as well.

These are not easy questions to answer, which is why the abortion debate can't be simplified into two opposing sides trading blows on a morally complex, politically tenuous battleground. Our personal stories are therefore critical to a deeper understanding of the realities of abortion, which are so much more complex than either side would like to admit. Unfortunately, the anti-abortion movement has been hugely successful in shaming and silencing women; subsequently, we rarely hear women's abortion stories, and we spend an enormous amount of energy defending a right that in a free society should be considered irrevocable. Particularly worrisome is the surprising fact that many women who terminate their pregnancies actually claim to oppose abortion. They feel justified in their own specific cases, but they view the other patients in the waiting room of the abortion clinic as "irresponsible" or "promiscuous." If women who have abortions themselves can't feel solidarity with one another, how can we begin to claim abortion as a legitimate, necessary, and moral option?

Speaking out and sharing our complex stories would highlight the nuances within the contested space where abortion resides. I share my own experience in large part to challenge the anti-choice assertion that all children conceived should be brought to term. Additionally, I'd like to dispel the myth that women who terminate their pregnancies are selfish or cruel. On the contrary, I believe my mother made a selfish choice by deciding to have and keep me. I'm sure she hoped that my dad would grow to love me, and she couldn't have known that he would be so cruel. Certainly my father is responsible for his behavior, and he could have accepted the challenge of fatherhood in a loving way, rather than punishing us. Yet, I still wonder if he might have treated us differently had we been born later, or had my mother been able to come clean with him about her desire to have children right away.

The decision to carry a pregnancy to term often comes down to both timing and money. If my brother and I had been born in France, my parents would have had access to resources to help ease the financial stress that resulted from my birth. For example, when one of my French cousins recently had a child, the government granted her over $1,000 to help prepare for the baby's arrival, covered the costs of her hospital stay, and is currently providing her with subsidies to help support her son. France has a number of other pro-natal policies, including extensive discounts for families similar to ones we see in this country for senior citizens (public transportation, movies, etc.). Since these benefits are given to every French citizen, the poor are not accused of draining the country's economic system. Though many complain about high taxes, they also value their strong welfare system and they fight to maintain it.

In sharp contrast, the United States has a significantly more punitive attitude toward families, specifically low-income families. Significant cuts to the welfare system have meant that as abortion has become more restricted, fewer women have access to government subsidies that cover prenatal care and other costs of raising children. Basic family-planning services, such as contraception and sex education, are increasingly less available to poor women; yet if these women carry their pregnancy to term, they face punitive measures in the form of welfare caps that limit financial support for the number of children they have, forcing them even further into poverty. Considering that many of the challenges of parenthood are connected to economics, it is hypocritical for the Bush administration to call itself "pro-life" when it advocates for economic and social policies that oppose the financial needs of low-income, working families.

It's telling that the states with the most abortion restrictions provide the fewest resources for family-planning services, prenatal care, and welfare programs for children. As such, we need to vociferously challenge the hypocrisy of an anti-abortion movement that claims to advocate for the unborn, yet actively lobbies against funding for family planning, education, health coverage, and welfare benefits. Instead of standing outside women's health clinics shaming women, those who oppose abortion would do better to fight for meaningful social change that would create a more supportive environment for families. No woman should be forced to bear a child she doesn't want or is not prepared to care for, nor should she be forced to abort a child she would have kept if only she had the necessary financial support.

While abortion will always remain a complex issue, my own experience as an unwanted child has shown me that the economic component is more important than even the reproductive rights movement generally acknowledges. Much of what I suffered growing up had to do with a lack of adequate resources, and my understanding of this dynamic as a teen led me to conclude that I should have been aborted rather than brought into the world under far-from-auspicious circumstances. I now understand how important the socioeconomic context is, and I can see that my childhood could have been much less painful had my parents chosen to stay in France. However, I'm sure that my father would have been emotionally unavailable no matter where I was raised, since his inadequacy as a parent did not solely originate with his financial troubles. However, I do believe that the United States could learn from countries with strong welfare systems and greater support for families, so that every woman has a real choice as to whether or not to bring a child into this world.

My story is full of ambiguities and ambivalence about my very existence, but my hope is that my perspective as a child only half-wanted can contribute to a deeper conversation about abortion within the pro-choice movement and elsewhere. In particular, I'd like to see a more honest and compassionate dialogue about how we conceptualize "the best interests of the child," so that our message is one of advocacy for women, children, and entire families. To that end, I believe that we must also continue to create space to work through the real-life consequences of our choices: for the women who grieve the loss of a child as well as the men; for those who are unprepared for the burdens of parenthood yet must suddenly assume responsibility for another's life, whether they choose to or not; and for the children who are brought into this world as well as the ones who are not. And further, my story is a call for a broader vision of reproductive rights, one that extends its focus beyond abortion and seeks to create alliances with other progressive causes, such as universal healthcare and welfare rights, so that we may build a truly holistic movement dedicated to social, economic, and reproductive justice. In this way, we can begin to envision a world where every child is indeed a wanted child, and families have the resources to care for each one of them.

UNSPOKEN LOSS
The Experience of "Therapeutic" and Late-Term Abortion
KRISTA JACOB

We felt that if our daughter had been in a car accident and was on life support with the same internal injuries, we would not keep her on life support and let her suffer. This child deserved the same dignity.

—A grieving mom*

I initially thought I would "be brave" and continue my pregnancy. But I came to realize that, ultimately, it wasn't about how strong I could be, how deeply I wanted this baby, or what important lessons he could teach me. It was about what he would experience in his short life. Given his diagnosis, he would have known only suffering. As his mother, I couldn't allow that to happen.

—A mother at peace*

IN MY WORK AS A REPRODUCTIVE HEALTH COUNSELOR, I FOUND that most women considering abortion assumed that their potential babies would be born full-term and healthy, without any genetic abnormalities. *I can't afford to raise a child right now. My relationship can't withstand the stress of another child. I need to finish college before I start a family. I don't have the resources to raise another child.* It was on rare occasion that I heard a woman or her significant other talk about the possibility that their potential baby might be born with a disability (or disabilities) as a factor in their decision-making. My colleagues referred to this as "stage one" thinking: If you can't care for a presumably healthy baby, then, for most, it's a given that you don't progress to the next stage and ask yourself other questions such as: *What would I do if there are serious genetic problems with my pregnancy? How would I support a child with serious disabilities? How would I feel about having a late-term abortion if it meant preserving my health or saving a potential baby from suffering?*

I often asked the couples I counseled who had decided, sometimes reluctantly, to continue their pregnancy, to imagine what it would truly be like to raise a child or to place their child for adoption. Were they prepared to fully commit to either option? What's more, I encouraged them to ask themselves even more difficult questions, such as how they might feel if they discovered there were genetic problems with the fetus, or if their child was born dangerously premature. Were they prepared to have a child with special needs, and if not, why? Though I affirmed that the majority of babies are born healthy, I encouraged them to consider these deeper questions because I believe that being pregnant, raising a child, and placing a child for adoption (as well as having an abortion) are monumental experiences that require profound thought and consideration. It isn't about anticipating all that can go wrong—that's impossible—but, from my experience, it's important to encourage people to go beyond the romanticization and mythical thinking that surrounds both pregnancy and parenthood in our culture, and to peel back all the layers that go into deciding if one is ready to be responsible for life.

People in the medical field, or those who may already have a disabled child, or who have had the experience of ending a pregnancy because of severe genetic or fetal problems, are aware of these risks because their lives have already been touched by the reality most of us try to keep at bay during pregnancy. It's understandable and, I suppose, natural that one might view a situation, even a very tragic one, in the most positive light. Life is often very difficult and would be more so if we were constantly anticipating the potential problems or the worst-case scenarios. In the case of a planned pregnancy, maybe one that was planned for years, it's an exciting and optimistic time, a time when most relish and revel in the possibilities of pregnancy. And if would-be parents receive the news that there are serious problems with their pregnancy, most are left feeling shock and confusion. In her essay "My Late-Term Abortion," Gretchen Voss reflected on her own feelings about pregnancy before she received the devastating news that her developing baby had a severe case of spina bifida and hydrocephalus: "Nobody told me that pregnancy was a gamble, not a guarantee. Nobody told me that what was rooting around inside me was a hope, not a promise."[1]

Many pregnant women also convince themselves that if they do all the right things before and during their pregnancy—if they don't drink alcohol or smoke cigarettes, if they take prenatal vitamins daily, and so on—their developing baby will automatically be healthy.

It was our ignorance for believing that all pregnancies led to a healthy baby. It was my arrogance for believing that since I had the best medical care, took prenatal vitamins even before and during my pregnancy, never took drugs, never smoked cigarettes, and drank about half a glass of wine a year, that our baby would be safe.

—A grieving mom*

Their denial, and perhaps blind optimism, makes them feel some degree of control in a circumstance over which they are powerless in many ways. Admittedly, healthy choices are critical to the developing embryo and fetus, but the genetic makeup is already determined when the zygote is formed. Genetic anomalies can happen to the most conscientious pregnant woman, just as healthy babies can be born to women who don't always make healthy choices. My doctor prescribed folic acid supplements for me when I was trying to conceive, which I took religiously, and after I became pregnant I adhered to all the standards for a healthy pregnancy. Yet, despite my knowledge about genetics and all the pregnancies I've seen go terribly wrong, there was some piece of me that attributed my choices to the fact that I gave birth to healthy children. I understand why a woman who learns that her baby has genetic problems (or otherwise) might draw a similar connection. In terms of genetics, it's a false connection, but nevertheless we draw it.

Among couples who receive the devastating news that there are fatal or severe problems with their pregnancy, many decide to terminate it. This procedure, often referred to as "therapeutic abortion," is done to save the life of the mother or to prevent suffering of the potential baby. Despite right-wing propaganda against these procedures, which they've manipulatively dubbed "partial-birth abortion," therapeutic abortions are not done for frivolous reasons and the decisions are not made lightly. In fact, many women feel that it is their only choice. Severe fetal anomalies can put the mother's health or life at risk, or cause serious fetal problems that are either incompatible with life or will cause eventual death. There are women and couples who decide that the best way to be responsible for their potential baby is to end the pregnancy.

A friend from college recently wrote to me. She'd heard that I was putting together a book about abortion and wanted to share her story. "My husband and I lost our unborn baby last year. We told everyone she died because of problems with her kidneys, but in reality she had Edwards syndrome. She would have been born extremely disabled and lived for only a short time. I couldn't do that to all of us, including our precious baby girl." I knew that Edwards syndrome (referred to as "Trisomy 18" in the medical community) is a fairly common syndrome that's caused by an extra chromosome on the eighteenth chromosomal pair. It leads to multiple health problems, including heart, renal, and respiratory failure, blindness, deafness, and severe mental retardation. Usually these complications prevent the baby from surviving past the first three or four months. "I couldn't give birth to a baby I couldn't hold and love. I would not allow them to stick her in a sterile medical environment with tubes and wires attached to machines. That's not decent, it's not right."

She had only told two other people the truth about what happened. When she asked her doctor for resources, he told her and her husband that it would be difficult to find people willing to talk about this experience because terminating a late-term pregnancy has compounded stigma. It's not like an early abortion, and my friend, in fact, refused to call it an abortion at all. "You are actually birthing a baby. It's not a five-minute procedure, and the paradigm is different: Birth is supposed to be about creating new life, and celebrating that life, but our experience was mired in grief, shame, and death." She also confessed that what she felt most guilty about was that she did not give her daughter the name they had originally decided upon. "I felt like I dishonored her by not giving her the name I had chosen for the healthy baby I had imagined I would have. To this day, I feel such remorse about it. If I could change anything it would be that I would have given her that name, that I would have honored her in that way, but now it's too late."

It's normal for people to revisit traumatic situations and find one aspect of their experience to which they assign all of their unresolved and painful feelings, some piece that exemplifies all of the feelings and emotions they haven't fully processed. For my friend, it was the fact that she gave her baby a "secondary" name, nominally reserving her first name for a future healthy daughter, and hence further invalidating her genetically flawed baby. More than any other aspect of this horrible experience, the issue of the name still haunted her, and it was this particularly painful aspect that she still cannot come to terms with.

I felt deep sadness for this couple. Not only because of the loss of their baby, but because they both had been traumatized, like anyone would be after the death of a child, and no one had offered them support services of any kind. Their doctor was kind and appeared nonjudgmental, but neither he nor any of his nurses offered the couple a counselor or an advocate, not anyone to sit down with to help them get through this experience. They felt completely alone and isolated, and isolation is pernicious because it fosters stigma, shame, self-blame, and hatred, and it functions to keep people from realizing that they are, in fact, not alone. Though late-term abortion is rare, it is reported that of the one million U.S. abortions each year, 2,200 are D&X (dilation and extraction) procedures, a termination procedure sometimes used in late-term abortions.[2] There are thousands of women and couples who have had similar experiences, yet no one told them how many other women have gone through the same thing. If their child had been killed in a car accident, or if she had died from leukemia, they most certainly would have been offered support services. Their loss would have been acknowledged and their pain would have been validated and honored. Instead, after they baptized and said goodbye to their daughter, they were sent home, alone, in silence. As my friend pointed out, the message in all of this was: You deserve to suffer because you chose this.

In contrast, I know another woman who went to Women's Health Care Services in Wichita, Kansas, for her late-term abortion after she discovered her baby's brain was developing outside of its skull and would suffer imminent death. There, she was treated with dignity and a horrible situation was made a bit more tolerable. The organization's website, www .drtiller.com says, "Kindness, courtesy, justice, love, and respect are the cornerstones of our patient-provider relationships," and also includes a quote from its medical director, Dr. George Tiller, "Women and families are intellectually, emotionally, spiritually, and ethically competent to struggle with complex health issues—including abortion—and come to decisions that are appropriate for themselves." Despite his compassionate approach and invaluable service to thousands of couples, his work comes with a great cost. In 1993, he was shot by a "pro-life" fanatic and is still a target of the most extreme and unrelenting harassment.

In March 2006, *The New York Times Magazine* featured a story on couples suing their doctors for what has been termed "wrongful birth" lawsuits. The plaintiffs in the cases argue that their doctors neglected to perform important prenatal tests, even when there were signs of potential problems, which would have screened for severe genetic disorders. These parents contend that if they had known their babies were going to be born with severe disabilities, they would have terminated their pregnancies (hence the "wrongful birth" terminology) and saved their children from a lifetime of pain and suffering.

If prenatal testing is offered so that options can be considered, will this actually bias people toward termination? And, if so, is that a bad thing? Or will the opposite scenario occur: With more attention paid to potential problems (and subsequent options), will there be more information and research on the experience of disabilities so that parents who choose to continue their pregnancies will have more information and options? These are questions about which reasonable people can disagree, but with three decades of vitriolic controversy surrounding the abortion issue, it's almost impossible to have any kind of public dialogue that is not dictated by political and religious agendas. But what is important are the questions these lawsuits raise. As Elizabeth Weil wrote in that magazine story, " . . . no regulations yet guide parents and doctors about fair reasons for terminating or going forward with particular births. Should it be okay to terminate deaf children? What about a blind one? How mentally retarded is too mentally retarded?"[3] Weil's incisive questions and copious analysis are a refreshing contribution to this debate. She herself faced this decision two years ago when she and her husband discovered, in her twenty-third week of pregnancy, that their child had contracted the cytomegalovirus (CMV), a serious problem that can cause blindness, deafness, and mental retardation. They chose to abort, which was the right decision for them at the time. I've heard many women, whether they've had early or late-term abortions, say that it's the uncertainties that are often the hardest to reconcile. Maybe everything would have worked out okay. Maybe the baby would have been healthier than we thought. Maybe the tests were wrong. Uncertainties are inherent to difficult decisions, but most people make the most loving decision they can with the information they've been given.

Early-term abortion is common, but late-term abortion is not. Therefore, there are fewer people who have a deeply personal, "flesh and blood" understanding—a comprehension that transcends religious and political dogma as well as shallow, self-righteous judgments—of what it means to find out your wanted baby has severe genetic problems. This presents a barrier to a broader societal understanding of and compassion for these cases. This lack of awareness, coupled with the manipulative rhetoric surrounding this issue, is dangerous because it puts extremist thinking and politics before women's health and safety. We need to shift the power from the political spin doctors to the actual medical doctors and their patients so that all can be better served.

I believe a first step in finding an effective solution is to create a climate in which people who have had therapeutic abortions feel safe and even empowered to tell their stories. Our interest in their stories should be genuine, not voyeuristic, and though I think it's tough to know with certainty what any given person would do in this kind of situation, there is value in trying to imagine what it would be like if you were in their shoes. Recently, several of my friends had a group discussion about their own stance on this issue. One woman had received inconclusive results on one of her prenatal tests, and though her baby was born healthy, she had chosen not to have an amniocentesis or any further testing. Since it was her first pregnancy, she felt that unless her life was at risk, she would continue her pregnancy. However, she admitted that if she already had a child, she would have given serious thought to termination. She felt that it would be a harder gamble to make if you were already raising a child. For myself, my relationship and financial security would be important factors in determining what I would do. It's easy for late-term abortion to serve as the mantle where the self-righteous hang their hat, but it's important to remember that the reality of the outcome always looks different when seen through a personal, rather than a theoretical, lens.

If we promote awareness about the fact that things can go terribly wrong in a pregnancy, it's also possible that people will think more about the possibility of genetic problems before they become pregnant, or during the early stages of pregnancy. These kinds of conversations, even in cases when they aren't necessary, will serve to make people more informed, more aware about themselves and their partner, and hence more adequately prepared for pregnancy and parenthood.

The excerpts from www.aheartbreakingchoice.com are reprinted by permission, and I thank the organization for their commitment to education and awareness.

Thank you to my friends for sharing their stories and giving me permission to share them with others. I have changed the details to protect their privacy.

ABORTION BY ANY OTHER NAME

VICTORIA TEPE, PhD

THE PROCEDURE THAT "PARTIAL-BIRTH ABORTION" PRETENDS TO describe—but doesn't—is more accurately referred to as the D&X (dilation and extraction) procedure, a method of abortion sometimes used to terminate late second- and third-trimester pregnancies. This procedure was pioneered by Dr. James McMahon in 1983, and in 1992 was described in a monograph written by Dr. Martin Haskell, an Ohio-based physician.[1] The D&X method of abortion is controversial in part because it involves collapsing the fetal skull to reduce its size before the fetus is extracted through the woman's cervix. This procedure is important because it reduces the risk of damage to the woman's cervix as well as other potential physical and emotional hardships associated with abortions after twenty-two weeks of pregnancy.

When anti-abortion activists first learned about this new surgical technique, they dubbed it "brain-suction abortion" and launched an intense campaign to ban its practice in the state of Ohio. Their first attempt to ban the D&X procedure was in 1995, through Ohio House Bill 135, which renamed the procedure "partial-birth feticide" and deemed its practice a second-degree felony. Then-governor George Voinovich (now a U.S. senator) was eager to sign the ban into law, and did so. House Bill 135 ultimately failed in court, but it marked the beginning of a successful and insidious public-relations campaign in which later-term abortions became equated with *all* abortions, regardless of gestational length, and the campaign subsequently fueled public discomfort with abortion in general. In the ten years since "partial-birth abortion" was first challenged in Ohio, thirty-one other state legislatures have passed similar or identical laws to that proposed by HB 135.

"Partial-birth abortion" bans routinely fail in court. Why? Because they claim to prohibit a certain type of medical procedure—so-called partial-birth abortion—but fail to provide the information necessary for physicians and surgeons to comply with the ban. Some "partial-birth abortion" bans are so vague that they could legally prohibit any form of abortion, even those very early in pregnancy, when the D&X procedure is not used.

In 1999, Rhode Island's assistant attorney general, Rebecca Partington, attempted to defend her state's ban on "partial-birth abortion" by offering as many as ten different definitions of the procedure. Even Partington's key witness, a physician who provides abortions, conceded that some doctors might find the ban confusing because of its vague language. Among other things, the Rhode Island law failed to specify whether the prohibition against "partial-birth abortion" should apply throughout the entire pregnancy or only after the fetus might be viable.

When asked to explain the law's ambiguity, Partington contended that the law was "intentionally broad" because if it were more specific, it "wouldn't apply to anything." Perhaps Partington recognized the challenges inherent in legislating medical practice. The D&X procedure was designed because of the need for safer abortion later in pregnancy. If legislators were able to define the D&X procedure in legally acceptable terms, physicians might simply modify their technique so that it no longer met the legal definition, thus circumventing the law. Perhaps Partington also understood that because the D&X procedure was not even practiced in her state, a "partial-birth abortion" ban would have no effect on the number of abortions performed unless the ban could be applied more liberally to all types of abortion at any stage of pregnancy.

To make matters worse, when anti-abortion lawmakers attempt to ban "partial-birth abortion," they typically refuse to include exceptions in the law for women whose health may be compromised by alternative methods of second- or third-trimester abortion (i.e., induced labor and delivery). Here again, the courts disapprove. Although the "pro-life" movement refuses to acknowledge that abortion is sometimes necessary to protect a woman's health, our nation's courts have consistently prioritized the need to protect a woman's health and survival. In 2000, the U.S. Supreme Court issued a critical ruling—*Stenberg v. Carhart*—which found a "partial-birth abortion" ban in Nebraska unconstitutional because it was vague and did not include exceptions for a woman whose health is threatened by continuing her pregnancy.

Though *Stenberg v. Carhart* laid to waste most "partial-birth abortion" bans, it also provided specific guidance for anti-choice legislators to craft a ban that could survive judicial scrutiny: First, the law must define "partial-birth abortion" very clearly and specifically in order to distinguish it from other forms of abortion; second, the law must include an adequate exception for its application when deemed necessary to protect a woman's health.

However, with few exceptions, state and national anti-choice legislators continued to write and pass "partial-birth abortion" statutes that contained intentionally vague language and no provision for protecting a woman's health. Most notably, the U.S. Congress passed, and President George W. Bush signed into law, the Partial-Birth Abortion Ban Act of 2003, which again failed to make an exception for the life or health of the pregnant woman. The Partial-Birth Abortion Ban Act has already been challenged successfully in the federal district and circuit courts. The Bush administration has appealed to the U.S. Supreme Court, which has agreed to hear the case (*Gonzales v. Carhart*) in 2006.

The irony of "partial-birth abortion" is that even a constitutionally acceptable "partial-birth abortion" ban (one that is clearly defined and acknowledges the need to protect a woman's health) would have no discernible impact on the number of abortions performed in the United States, or specifically on the number of late-term abortions. Almost nine of every ten abortions occurs during the first trimester of pregnancy, when the D&X procedure is not used.[2] Abortions in the third trimester are already extremely rare (1.5 percent of abortions occur after twenty weeks of pregnancy) because very few states permit third-trimester abortions and very few women want or need to have an abortion so late in a pregnancy.[3] Thus, a law that specifically bans the use of the D&X procedure would affect only a very small percentage of women in need of an abortion during the late second trimester (between twenty-one and twenty-four weeks of gestation). Yet, this is not to say that a ban on D&X abortion would have no effect. The women who are the most grateful for the D&X procedure are those whose *wanted* pregnancies have gone tragically wrong. The D&X method of abortion has enabled some of these women and their families to minimize suffering and avoid illness, injury, and/or extensive medical intervention that can result from pregnancies involving fetuses that are very sick, severely deformed, dying, or already lifeless. For the small number of women and families in this uniquely difficult circumstance, a ban on the D&X procedure would have deeply tragic effects.

Anti-abortion activists understand that a national ban on third-trimester abortions generally would have very little, if any, impact on overall abortion rates. They lobby to ban a particular type of abortion not because they hope to have any real impact on the rate or number of abortions in the United States, nor even because they expect to prevent some small number of late-term abortions, but rather because the "partial-birth abortion" debate provides an invaluable opportunity to portray all abortions as grotesque and brutal. Simply put, the "partial-birth abortion" debate is a public-relations ploy. Conservative Republicans execute this cynical strategy as an opportunity to placate anti-abortion lobbyists and activists whose campaign contributions are essential to their political survival.

As a matter of politics and public relations, the nationwide effort to ban "partial-birth abortion" has been enormously successful for one reason only: As human beings, we find it difficult, if not impossible, to imagine that the D&X procedure—or any other form of abortion, for that matter—is a painless experience for the fetus. It is this assumption of pain and suffering that makes "partial-birth abortion" a seemingly obvious act of brutality. Absent the question of fetal pain, the D&X procedure could not be characterized as more or less "grotesque," "barbaric," or "inhumane" than any other form of abortion. These are the disturbing descriptors that fuel public discomfort and disapproval over late-term abortion. Were it known for a fact that the fetus felt nothing, no single abortion procedure would seem more or less disturbing than any other. The anti-abortion movement has used and will continue to use "partial-birth abortion" to make the persistent and usually effective demand that we equate abortion with pain.

The debate about "partial-birth abortion" does raise legitimate questions that relate to fetal development, fetal capacity, and fetal viability. Regardless of how activists on either side of the debate feel about these issues, questions surrounding fetal development are nonetheless relevant and important to ordinary citizens, legislators, and judges. Women who seek abortions often express genuine concern that "the baby" might suffer.

The question of fetal pain is an unavoidable issue in our effort to reconcile social policy and legislation that every woman can live with or, if abortion becomes re-criminalized, might die without. We don't have to demonstrate that abortion is painless in order to defend its constitutionality, but we would be smart to address proactively the issue of fetal pain, one way or another.

There is no clear scientific consensus concerning when or how the human fetus experiences pain. In fact, there is no clear consensus on how to define the capacity to feel pain, nor even a majority opinion on how best to identify or measure the conscious experience of pain in individuals who cannot communicate. Because pain is a complicated and essentially physiological process, it is wrong to assume that the capacity for pain exists as soon as all the necessary anatomical "hardware" is in place. What is not known by medical science is precisely how various regions of the brain work together to support the conscious experience of pain. Hormonal and chemical changes that often occur in response to pain or stress can be seen in children and adults who report feeling no pain at all. Exaggerated reflexive responses in premature infants might indicate sensitivity to pain, or might instead suggest the presence of a primitive system, the very purpose of which is to protect an organism that is otherwise unable to feel, avoid, or respond to pain.

By asking different questions and using different research techniques, scientists who perform pain research have reached different conclusions. Some believe that the fetus may be capable of responding to pain as early as thirteen weeks, while others believe that the conscious experience of pain depends on higher-order brain development and function that doesn't occur until very late in pregnancy, or even after birth.

For all this apparent disagreement, we can reach sensible, if conservative, conclusions concerning *if* and *when* the human fetus might experience pain. The basic "hardware" or structures for pain transmission—peripheral nerves, spinal cord, and brain stem—begin to develop very early in pregnancy, but are not fully developed until well into the second trimester or early in the third. We do not know if this means the fetus experiences pain sensation, but it is reasonable and cautious to suppose that such an experience may be *possible* sometime between twenty-six and thirty weeks of gestation.

Perhaps the more relevant question is *how* the fetus experiences pain. Some studies suggest that while premature infants do experience pain, their experience of pain occurs more slowly than in full-term infants, children, and adults. Fetuses' biochemical responses to painful events may be delayed due to slower transmission of information to the brain. If so, faster methods of abortion, such as the D&X procedure, might circumvent the pain problem by causing the fetus to die more quickly than its nervous system can effectively transmit sensory information to the brain. So-called "partial-birth abortion" might actually be more humane and more merciful than slower, alternative procedures such as in-utero dismemberment or saline-induced abortion.

No matter how much we know (or don't know) about fetal pain, it is important to remember that abortions late in pregnancy often involve fetuses that are already in extreme physical distress, or whose brains and nervous systems are already severely compromised, or women whose health is threatened by pregnancy. These tragic circumstances are consistently ignored in the anti-abortion rhetoric about "partial-birth abortion."

Opponents of abortion and their representatives in Congress walk a fine line when they single out one method of abortion as worse than any other. Their efforts imply that other methods of abortion are in some way better, preferable, or more acceptable than "partial-birth abortion." If a law prohibits just one method of abortion, that's all it does. And if the effort to ban "partial-birth abortion" were legally successful, it would quickly become obvious to the courts—and to the public—that the anti-abortion movement is unwilling to settle for such a limited victory. Leaders of the anti-abortion movement will not rest until abortion is re-criminalized at all stages of pregnancy. Those most dedicated to the anti-abortion cause also oppose emergency contraception and many forms of birth control.

Most disturbing is that so-called pro-life politicians invoke "partial-birth abortion" to divert attention away from more obvious questions that any serious and sincere person should want to raise: *Why* do women seek abortions late in pregnancy? And what can we do to help them avoid that need? Answers to these questions would reveal duplicity on the part of lawmakers who oppose late-term abortion and at the same time support laws that make it more difficult for women to find, afford, and receive safe abortion care early in their pregnancies. Rather than making abortion safer or more humane, restrictions such as mandatory waiting periods and parental-consent laws create cumbersome obstacles and delays that force some women to have later abortions. These delays could make a critical difference in the development of the fetal nervous system. The D&X procedure exists because some abortions do take place later in pregnancy.

"Partial-birth abortion" exists to keep us from wondering why.

THE POLITICS OF FETAL PAIN

ALISSA PERRUCCI

LEGISLATION ON THE PREVENTION OF FETAL PAIN DURING ABORTION was introduced in 2005 in both the U.S. Congress and the Senate and thus took its place in the long line of post-*Roe* regulations that have aimed to increase barriers to women who want access to abortion services. The issue of fetal pain is a powerful emotional issue that the anti-abortion movement works to embrace because it invokes images of fetal suffering. Like the deliberate reframing of intact dilatation and extraction (D&X) as "partial-birth abortion," the fetal pain issue is an attempt on the part of those who are against abortion to reinforce the image of barbarism in the abortion procedure.

The Unborn Child Pain Awareness Act was introduced in January 2005 in the House (HR 356, sponsored by Representative Christopher Smith, R-N.J.) and the Senate (S 51 sponsored by Senator Sam

Brownback, R-Kans.). The stated purpose of the bill was to increase patient awareness of the possibility that the fetus may experience pain during termination. It required physicians performing abortions at or after twenty weeks of gestation to read a script—crafted by members of Congress—to the patient, wherein the physician must offer the patient pain medication for the fetus during the abortion, or provide the woman with a referral to a physician who would.

The merit of the bill was contested on scientific grounds. The debate centered on whether or not the fetus had the physiological capacity to experience pain. In an article in the August 2005 issue of the *Journal of the American Medical Association*, researchers (an attorney and four physicians) concluded from a meta-analysis that it was unlikely that a fetus experienced pain in the same manner as an adult human prior to twenty-nine weeks of gestation.[1] The paper also pointed out that it was doubtful that the reflex response of the fetus was equal to our psychological and physiological perception of pain. To complicate matters further, the authors indicated that even in conditions where fetal pain was a possibility, the success of different methods by which pain-reducing medications would be delivered to a fetus could not be fully determined. Most worrisome, however, was that fetal anesthesia might greatly increase the risk of medical complications for the woman, and thus extend the amount of time necessary to complete the abortion procedure.

The article's conclusions angered opponents of abortion, but the ensuing hysteria clouded an issue that should have aroused concern in all Americans. In S 51/HR 356, Congress took a definitive stance in an area of science that is, at best, incomplete, and dictated to physicians the parameters of caring for and advising their patients. Regardless of the medical scenario, the health and well-being of the patient is compromised when physicians are no longer able to determine the appropriate course of treatment for their patients.

The patronizing language contained in the script that the physician was obligated to read to the patient is cause for serious concern. It revealed a thinly veiled aim to introduce shame, anxiety, and guilt into a woman's decision-making process. It did not, as some argued, serve to augment informed consent. Indeed, the fetus was referred to as the "pain-capable unborn child." In an incongruous and dispassionate tone, the words of Congress advised that "the process of being killed in an abortion" would cause the fetus pain, constituting the fetus as *someone experiencing something*. Finally, Congress essentially stated that the fetus would experience pain during the abortion, in reminding the patient in clear language, "even though *you* [emphasis is mine] received a pain-reducing drug or drugs." Situated within the language of this script, a patient refusing fetal pain medication would appear to be something akin to a sociopath.

An authentic informed-consent process is not achieved by the use of inflammatory language that equates the fetus with a born child or that implies that abortion is the same as killing a born person. These are personal beliefs, not facts. Moreover, the script informed the patient that an agent other than the physician, i.e., Congress, had rendered medical judgment on this issue. It did not matter whether the physician—the expert—agreed or disagreed. This insertion of Congress's beliefs into medical consultation undermines the collaborative process between the physician and the patient.

At the time of this writing, three states have enacted mandated informed-consent laws that require women seeking abortions to be offered the opportunity to review information on fetal pain. Disguised in the language of feminism, these laws are known as the "Woman's Right to Know Act." States have created websites with information and images of fetal development claiming that at twenty weeks' development, the fetus has the physiological capacity to experience pain, as evidenced by the reflex response. The language equates the stimulus-response behavior of the fetus with that of the born child and adults. It also reminds women that during fetal surgery, fetuses ("unborn children") are administered pain medication.

There would be numerous negative repercussions if S 51/HR 356, or any future iteration of this bill, became law. The already miniscule number of second-trimester abortion providers would dwindle. Few physicians would be able to provide the complex procedure of fetal anesthesia, even if Congress settled upon acceptable methods of delivery. Others would simply refuse to be mandated by law to practice medicine in a manner that could increase the risks to the health and life of the patient.

These negative repercussions, however, are unlikely to arouse the sympathy of the public. The public's discomfort with late-term abortion will trump images of desperate women seeking second-trimester abortions for fetal anomaly or because they didn't discover they were pregnant in the first trimester. The public will not be moved by the stories of women whose abortions were pushed into the second trimester because of failures of the medical system: women who discover that they are sixteen weeks pregnant but only have enough money to pay for the rent *or* for the abortion; women who drive five hours to a clinic and discover that they are thirteen weeks pregnant and the nearest clinic only provides abortions up to twelve weeks; or women given the runaround from anti-abortion healthcare professionals who didn't inform them that they were eligible for public assistance for their abortions in states where this is an option. Research shows that other legislative efforts mandating that patients meet certain requirements before they can obtain an abortion have the additional consequence of delaying abortions. For minors seeking abortions in states with parental-involvement laws, the process of obtaining a judicial bypass can delay the abortion for two to four days[2] or past the eighth week of pregnancy.[3] Similarly, after the twenty-four-hour mandatory delay law went into effect in Mississippi, there was an increase in the proportion of second-trimester abortions to state residents.[4]

Anti-choice politicians, legislators, and activists want women to suffer and pay penance for getting pregnant. Women echo this sentiment when they condemn their peers for "laying down with a man" and proclaim that their rightful punishment is having the baby. In the clinic, counselors often hear this same rhetoric coming out of the mouths of anti-abortion women who demand to have an abortion, but who are able to separate themselves from the "other women" in the waiting room. Abortion is okay for them in this instance, but not for others because "they" aren't behaving as solemnly as they should be or because "they" appear to be from a lesser social or spiritual class.

For legislators of mandated consent laws, the objective is to introduce information into the decision-making process that shames the pregnant woman and passes judgment on her choice to have an abortion. These laws are disguised in the pro-choice language of empowering the patient with facts that will help her make a better decision. Unspoken but implied is that the better decision is to leave the clinic and carry the pregnancy to term. These mandated consent scripts do not aim to make the woman better informed—they strive to persuade her to decide against abortion. If they fail in these attempts, they have planted the seeds of guilt and shame that they hope will last a lifetime.

The purpose of authentic informed consent in the medical context is threefold: to communicate (1) the nature and purpose of the treatment; (2) its risks and benefits; and (3) any available alternatives to the treatment proposed.[5] Physicians determine which information is pertinent for patients, distinguish too much information from too little, put that information in context, and decide *how* to communicate the information to the patient. Physicians *already* address the issue of fetal pain when a patient initiates the conversation, and accommodate the patient's requests —including the request for pain medication that may affect the fetus.

An authentic informed-consent process also acknowledges that it is not perfect—that it is impossible to discuss all the possible risks and benefits to every procedure because there are infinite consequences to every choice that we make. Would Congress want to introduce legislation to require physicians to discuss the possible *benefits* of abortion over childbirth and adoption? Or would Congress want to require obstetricians to read a script to patients prior to childbirth regarding the prevalence of postpartum psychosis or the negative effects of maternal depression on children's psychosocial and cognitive development?

A more exhaustive informed-consent process in the context of unintended pregnancy would also require that society recognize the possibility that abortion can be a responsible choice. The life situations in which this designation might occur are infinite, but the specifics are, in the end, irrelevant. What matters is that whatever decision a woman makes with respect to her pregnancy must be *her* decision. Women already have the freedom to discuss fetal pain with their physicians, whether the discussion involves scientific evidence or personal feelings and beliefs. And in every instance that a patient is concerned about fetal pain during her abortion, the concern is, categorically, a legitimate one.

In the abortion procedure, the patient that is entrusted to the physician's care is the woman, not the fetus. It is a moral imperative that the health, life, and well being of the woman take precedence. The intent of mandated informed-consent laws is to complicate rather than facilitate a medical decision and procedure, and they directly conflict with the physician's goal of caring for the patient. Ultimately, physicians must have the autonomy and authority to consult with their patients in a manner that is consistent with their medical training and with scientific evidence. When engaged in the informed-consent process, they must first have the goal to do no harm. Then they can empower the patient by providing her with the information that allows her to make the best possible decision for her life and for herself.

ABORTION CLINIC DAYS

"BON" AND "LOU"

"IF PEOPLE JUST KNEW THE REALITY OF PEOPLE'S ABORTION STORIES and situations like we do, it could really shift things," Bon said—a familiar lament when abortion providers get together. On this occasion, in the fall of 2003, Bon was responding to something Lou had mentioned to her after having just read an article about blogs in *The New York Times*. The article captured Bon's and Lou's (not their real names) imaginations that weekend, and they began the process of envisioning a website where they could speak from their hearts and talk honestly about what happens in an abortion clinic. Together, they created the following mission:

> *The purpose of our blog site is to provide a safe place to talk freely about our work, our patients' stories, and how we feel about the experience of*

abortion in this country. We have chosen to remain anonymous because we want to talk about the "real stuff" without censoring ourselves.

Their first challenge came from a reader—an "anti"—who accused the authors of violating women's confidentiality. "That took me aback," confessed Bon, "and, initially, it made me less enthusiastic about writing the hard stuff and more cautious about revealing details." It also put them squarely in the same place as the women and men they were writing about: in the middle of a maddeningly ignorant debate. "It made me even more committed to getting our stories out there," said Lou, "and I think we have struck a chord with a lot of people who write us to say, 'Thank you for who you are and what you report.'" The silver lining about catching the attention of the anti-abortion Internet forces is that the site ranks high in Google's results for "abortion clinics."

Here are a few of the dozens of blog entries written by Bon and Lou on www.abortionclinicdays.com:

The Importance of Bonding

Yesterday, a couple just back from the Iraq War had decided that for them and for their family, the pregnancy could not continue. The woman—I'll call her Rosa—was sent to Iraq when her baby was only six months old. Her husband was already there. Although they pleaded with the Army, they were told that no exceptions could be made. Of course, Rosa became very depressed in Iraq as a result of being away from her baby, a separation that lasted for an entire year. But she felt fortunate, too, that her mother was able to care for her baby. She had heard stories from others who had been told to put their babies in foster care.

Now both Rosa and her husband are back in the United States and she is in counseling for the depression that began a year ago when she was separated from her daughter. Rosa and her husband are trying to get to know one another again, trying to put together the life that crumbled when they were sent to Iraq. Their daughter does not know them and she clings to her grandmother, the only "mother" she knows.

They were using birth control because the last thing either of them wanted was another baby; however, their birth control failed. They believe their focus needs to be on reestablishing a relationship with their daughter and creating a stable home before having another child. They consulted a child psychologist who agreed that bringing another child into their home would not be a good idea. They strongly felt, and their psychologist agreed, that they needed to repair the bond with their baby that had been disrupted when they left for Iraq.

So, Rosa and her husband have come to our clinic today to do the best thing for their daughter. They thought about their decision for a long time and concluded that they could not bring another child into their home without further damaging the one they have, since their relationship with her is still so fragile. They want her to get to know them and they want to get to know her, too. Abortion was chosen out of love for their child.

—Lou

"I Was Blind . . . "

One of the women who captured my heart this week was a Latina—I will call her Mariana—who came to the clinic with her eight-month-old baby and her sister. We always ask patients not to bring their children. I wish we had a separate waiting room for them, but we don't. After I told her this, she offered to reschedule her appointment. But I could tell that she was ambivalent about her decision to have an abortion, so we did an ultrasound and determined she was eight weeks pregnant, which would give her plenty of time to reconsider her options. We then sat down for a counseling session.

Because it was the beginning of the day and I had a lot of ultrasounds to do and patients to counsel, I thought I would simply confirm that she would think about her decision further and come back if she wanted to have an abortion. By now, I should know better that it isn't this simple.

Mariana needed to tell her story. She already has a nine-year-old daughter from a previous relationship. She was introduced to this current fellow by a friend. She got pregnant on the first date, which resulted in her now eight-month-old. "So you didn't really know him long?" I interjected. "Right," she responded. However, he is devoted to her and to the baby that she felt she should have; abortion had not been much of a consideration for her then. The big problem now is that he is mean to her oldest child, the one that is not his. It is also clear that he is very controlling of her and he is taking advantage of her financially. "I was blind," she said, "and now I don't know how to get out of it." Understandably, she was concerned about having a second child with him, and that "then maybe I'll never get out."

The problem? "I am against this sort of thing: abortion and adoption. Last time, my mother said, 'You will have it. We don't do things like abortion.' " This time, her mother said the same thing, but apparently without as much conviction. Her sister supports her, but is worried how she will do afterwards. "You're different from me," she said. "You're more sensitive and it would be hard on you." She, too, was worried about how she would cope. "Do women have a hard time after?" she asked.

"Well, that depends, of course," I said, but that was not the answer she needed to hear. We talked about how her first responsibility is to her children, especially to her eldest, who was suffering. Could her boyfriend change his heart or his behavior? She thought not; she had tried to talk to him, begged him to change. How would she feel about adoption? It turns out her sister could not conceive; could she give her child to her sister? Not without his legal permission, I pointed out. Could she sacrifice this pregnancy—this beginning of life, for her other two children and for herself and feel that she was doing "the least bad" thing? She would think about that.

So, she left with a workbook* tucked under her arm, feeling better for having had the chance to talk to someone, and with a lot of hard work ahead of her. She shook my hand and thanked me.

—Bon

Family Values

I spent some time with a woman this week, once just for talking and then when she came in for an abortion. "Juliana" is Latina and African American, has two children, and is about eleven to twelve weeks pregnant. Her older son is a teen and her younger son, "my baby" as she calls him, is five years old and has been diagnosed with autism. He was fine until age three, completely verbal and on track developmentally. They think a vaccination caused his autism, but Juliana didn't really know much about the cause of it—just that he needs a lot of attention beyond his specialized schooling.

Juliana's current partner is against abortion, but he also says that if they ever split up (which seems likely) he would try to get custody of the child, or he might just "grab it." Suddenly she is seeing him differently. Still, she would like to believe in the best outcome: that he will stick around, that she will have a little girl, an unblemished child. When she talks like this, her voice gets very soft and her look is far away, and then it's almost as if she shakes herself back to reality.

"My son needs me," she states simply. "When my little niece is around, he can't bear sharing me." Juliana may have a fantasy about a family, but she chooses the needs of her sons over and over again. She has hope that her sons will grow with her attention and love.

---

*Now standard counseling issue. It can be found at www.pregnancyoptions .info.

Sometimes, or actually often, valuing family means choosing abortion. That's, unfortunately, a well-kept secret.

—Bon

Shifting Gears

It is such a satisfying moment, as a counselor, to witness a patient's internal shift. It is mostly a matter of having time to let the woman just talk about her situation, although sometimes when I ask a good question, or make an accurate observation, or give her some encouragement, it helps her realize her inner wisdom more quickly.

I was very fortunate the other day to have two such profound moments back-to-back, with very different outcomes, and I was able to actually see, hear, and feel a shift in each woman's understanding of her choices.

"Adrienne" was very poised. She was in graduate school, the daughter of a single mother who had sacrificed a lot to raise her. Her partner was very much against her having an abortion, and I had the feeling that he had pushed her into having intercourse in the first place. She was very religious and wrote on her form that she was concerned that she was "losing God." It turned out that her partner was having his "spiritual advisors" (friends from the Bible seminary he attended) call her a lot, and that he was telling her that God would be mad at her, that she would go to hell, and that God would not want her anymore. When she came to me, she was crying but still able to talk about her situation; her eyes kept overflowing with giant tears.

Adrienne spoke eloquently about her mother and all that her mother had lost in the many sacrifices she made for her. She was hoping for a better balance in her own life between becoming the educator she hoped to be and having children, both of which she wanted very much. A closer look at her support system also revealed some things that she didn't like about her partner, who was saying so many negative and hurtful things.

We talked a great deal about her religious beliefs and her relationship with God. I—no biblical scholar—reminded her of the biblical passage about how nothing "will be able to separate us from the love of God." (Romans 8, it turns out.) Finally, she sat up straighter and said, "God is still with me, I know that! I'm not going to let anyone convince me otherwise!" That was the first shift I witnessed, and I could see some internal alignment that often signifies resolution about a decision; where before her face was distorted with emotion, it became determined and at peace.

The second woman, "April," came in after several hours' driving to our clinic with the growing realization that she did not want an abortion. "The closer I got to here, the more I realized I didn't want an abortion," she said. I agreed, but was curious how she had gotten this far along in her decision. So we talked for some time, particularly about her previous pregnancy. April had a really terrible time and both she and the baby almost died toward the end. She said that she never wanted to go through that again. As April talked, though, it became clearer that underlying that difficult pregnancy was a deeper tragedy—her then-partner, an abusive and impetuous man, died in an accident after a fight with her. She had gone into premature labor. April felt responsible for his death, but she was also furious with him; and yet, she hadn't realized it until she contemplated ending this pregnancy. Quite suddenly, her posture and facial expression changed from one of perplexed agony to one of a centered, slightly abashed woman. "Oh, I guess I have been taking that anger out on this sweet man who could not be more different. He has refused to tell me what to do this whole time." Her regular therapist had told her as much, she reported, but she had not understood it until she was telling this story.

For both women, understanding how they had reached their present situation helped them to their own decision and brought them some kind of peace and resolve that had not been evident before. And I had the thrill of being there to help and to bear witness. I love my job!

—Bon

God Talk

Religion, God, faith, morality, ethics, etc., come up a lot at an abortion clinic, which may be a surprise to some people. For me, it's a fascinating look into what's important to people, how they make decisions, what guides their lives, and so on.

This week I have engaged in a lot of "God talk." One woman wrote "God" in the blank space provided for the preprinted question, "I am concerned about my relationship with _____." She was worried about punishment and retribution, but was trying to believe that God was compassionate and forgiving. This was a very matter-of-fact internal dialogue for her. Another, who identified herself as Christian, was very active in her church. Before the abortion she said, "I'm in church six days a week, yet here I am." She said that her religion forbids abortion, but after a good conversation she said that maybe her church was "too comfortable" in its position against abortion. She thought maybe they needed to examine the aspects of the issue that they weren't comfortable with. Even though she was steeped in her religion and its teachings, she knew in her heart that she was making the right choice. Life events, which included the cruelest of betrayals, made her see the abortion issue more clearly.

But the most compelling situation of all was that of a Mormon woman with whom I spent some time. Her beliefs on abortion were quite black and white—it was wrong and she would pay for it. But her husband did not want more kids (they had six) and though she was deeply saddened and would have sacrificed anything for her kids, including this one that currently measured the size of a pencil dot, she was going along with the abortion.

"Doesn't this put you in peril?" I asked. I think she was surprised at my question, but it seemed worth pointing out that doing something like this for your man, when you believed that you were jeopardizing your place in eternity, might not be a good idea. She remained firm in her desire to terminate her pregnancy no matter what I said, and she seemed quite willing to bear the consequences.

With women who are in spiritual or emotional distress, but refuse to be sent home to further consider their decision, I always try to talk about grief resolution. I offer the woman some ideas for saying goodbye to the pregnancy, or honoring the little life, or whatever makes sense to her within the context of her religion. In the case of the Mormon woman, baptism wasn't an option because Mormons don't believe children know right from wrong until age eight, which is when they are finally baptized. She wasn't looking for any quick fixes to make herself feel better.

In fact, comfort (even in the form of good pain medication) was not something she was interested in. Not knowing much about the Church of Latter-Day Saints, I asked how one is supposed to deal with a transgression of this magnitude in the church. She said that several days of prayer were required, and that when you were truly sorry, and sure you would not do it again, you needed to confess to the bishop. He would then either excommunicate you forever or he would "dis-fellow" you, which meant you could not receive the sacraments of the Church for a prescribed period of time.

After an ultrasound, which made it clear that her pregnancy was not even viable (she had a blighted ovum which would not grow), she was still clear that she would go to the Bishop and confess, "because I would have had the abortion no matter what . . . " There was something determined, steely almost, about her thinking on this matter. The Church was her life and she would do whatever was required of her, up to, and including losing her Church.

I don't know if this was courage or a need for punishment, but I do know that talking authentically about her situation was a good thing for her. It gave her some strength, and actually, she got through the abortion pretty well. She was okay afterwards, and she drove herself home— over two hours away.

She may still think that she is the only Mormon who has had an abortion, but at least she didn't feel completely alone. That's keeping my faith.

—Bon

Spirit Child

One of the everyday realities of my job is that there is no language for the experiences we are talking about. In the dialogues I have with patients, it is an ongoing process to find ways to express difficult concepts and feelings, like "soul" and "spirit." Sometimes, like today, I can serve as the bridge between two women and their experience of abortion.

The woman I counseled had two children already and, although she felt sad and guilty about it, "Rita" was quite sure that this was not the right time to bring another child into the world. Finances, other kids, emotional health, and the amount of time she could devote to her kids and her own pursuits all played into her decision to have an abortion. Rita was sure about her decision, but she was struggling to express something that she could not quite articulate. "I'm not sure I'm ready to say goodbye," she said. We talked about her decision and how to find a way to honor this loss, chosen though it may be. I went through my usual litany of ways that others had found to honor this experience. Finally, she said, a little tentatively, "Do you think souls can come back?"

"I don't know that anyone can ever know that," I said gently, "but let me tell you what another woman told me. She was a woman who meditated on her decision for a long time. Finally, after much thought, she reported that she felt that she was able to talk to the 'spirit child' that she was carrying. She told it how sorry she was that she could not have it. The 'spirit child' said to her, 'Don't worry, I'm a spirit, I can return in any form, at any time.'" I remember vividly how at peace that woman was with this spiritual comfort. Hearing this story gave Rita a new lens through which to examine her spiritual question.

After she had the abortion, she asked to see the pregnancy tissue that came out of her. She was five weeks pregnant (three weeks gestation), so there was only a tiny translucent sac floating on water. She touched the glass dish and said, "I love you. Come back when I'm ready."

As I write this, I can feel all sorts of people—from anti-abortion pundits to pragmatic skeptics—gearing up for some cynical polemic. And I want to hold up my hands and say, "Wait! Don't criticize what these women have come up with to express their innermost thoughts." What they are trying to express is very personal and tender and important. What one woman finds to speak her heart may hold the key for all of us to understand this complicated, paradoxical view of life. And their language will illuminate us all.

—Bon

Making It Up

Waiting rooms are difficult places to be, especially for guys. Today I met a young man I'll call Raymond who really caught my eye. His foot was jittery with nerves. As I talked to "Gloria," his girlfriend or ex-girlfriend, as it turned out, he made it clear that he too wanted to talk with me. After she and I established that she was sure of her decision, he joined us. He said, "If you hadn't called me in just now, I think I would have run out." He had talked on his cell phone to a relative who agreed with him that he was not ready to be a dad, but it was still a difficult and emotional decision for him—for both of them—but she was much more resolved and knew where she wanted to be in her life.

Just before I was about to send him back to the dreaded waiting room, I asked, "Any questions or things you want to say?" "Well . . . " he stammered, "What, uh, do you, uh, do, uh, with it?" "Good question." I answered. "We cremate—burn it." He nodded, and asked, "Well, this is going to sound really crazy, but, uh, could I . . . see [the fetal tissue]?" I responded, "Yes, with Gloria's permission—if you want to see it, either of you can. In fact, if you want to put something in with it—a note, a flower, whatever, you can." Gloria said she absolutely did not want to look at it, but Raymond said he did.

It turned out that Gloria changed her mind and looked at the fetal tissue after the abortion. Her pregnancy was about nine weeks or so, and you could just make out the fetus, about an inch long. We wash it off, rinse off any blood or clots, and float it in water—that helps to distinguish the placental tissue from the decidual tissue (the lining of the uterus). You can usually start to see a fetus at about nine weeks LMP (Last Menstrual Period, meaning from the first day of the last period), even though you can see it on ultrasound earlier than that.

I showed it to Raymond separately. He was quite agitated and teary, but he kept saying, "Thank you for showing it to me." We talked a bit about what he could take away from this experience, and I told him he would be a great dad when the time came (he was only nineteen) and I meant it. He was open and sweet. He said, "I thought it would be so easy, but it's not." Then he said, "Wait a minute. Can you wait for me?" He ran outside and got a flower and put part of it in with the fetus and said, "This part stays with me. I will always keep it." Then he crossed himself and kissed his fingers in goodbye gesture. He seemed calmer, again thanked me, and said, "I'll be okay."

I don't want anyone to think that these impromptu rituals are common, because they are not and they are not right for everyone. The interest has to come from the people involved—you wouldn't show someone fetal tissue if they didn't want to see it, for example. But usually it is very reassuring for patients since many think the embryo or fetus is as big as the pictures in the pro-life posters. There was a patient who put cigarette tobacco in with the tissue (a Native American tradition "to ease the trip to the other side") and another who wrote a note of love that we put in with the fetus.

I wish there were more opportunities inside (and beyond) the clinic to acknowledge the loss of a pregnancy if someone feels sad about the loss. Or maybe a ritual just to acknowledge the challenge of doing a hard thing and having feelings about it. The truth is that a lot of people do these kind of made-up rituals, and they provide them with some comfort. It feels scary for me to talk about it for fear of people misunderstanding, so I imagine it really feels scary for those patients who actually do it. I think individual women and men are very brave in facing all the negative talk about abortion. Often they know they made the right choice, but they also know it wasn't easy, and it's okay if they feel sadness. Complex feelings don't make good sound bites, and I know it's likely even these words will get distorted by anti-abortion forces. But I just thought people would appreciate the real, sometimes raw, emotion of some of the young men we meet.

—Bon

Cultural Differences

Sometimes I see a patient whose life experiences are so very different from mine, so different from anything I have ever even imagined, that I have to be conscious to look at her situation without any preconceived notions. I cannot even begin to genuinely hear what she needs to tell me until I can also understand a little about her life-shaping experiences.

"Tran" was born in Vietnam in the middle of the Vietnam War. Food, family, even being alive the next day were not things one could take for granted. She lost everything in her life before she was five years old: her parents, her village, her future. She was placed in a refugee camp yet somehow, and despite her sister's pleas to keep her in Vietnam, she found her way to America as a young adult.

Tran and her husband have created an existence for themselves that allows them to raise two children, sponsor various relatives to come to this country, and support a number of other people still living in Vietnam. They do so willingly and happily; it seems to give them great joy that their hard work helps so many people to have a better life.

When Tran came in today for her fifth abortion, a number of staff members were visibly and audibly agitated. They clearly were upset that all of the previous discussions about birth control appeared to have fallen on deaf ears. Tran said that she had tried the Pill after one of her children was born, but she discovered that she could not sleep while she was taking it. She also had developed facial pigmentation so that method was out. One by one, we went down the list of birth control methods, and she gave reasons why they did not work for her. In truth, what she wants is to have her tubes tied (a tubal ligation), but she has no medical insurance, works in her store twelve hours a day, six days a week, and can neither afford to take time off nor to pay for the surgery.

Tran clearly wishes that her unplanned pregnancies had not occurred, but she says that she is sure that "Buddha knows [her] heart." I do not know enough about Buddhism to converse with her much about it, but, as she pointed out, neither does she. She has her own religion that includes three days of Bible reading after each abortion because she wants her babies to go to heaven. In addition, she says that each time she goes to Vietnam, she buys a thousand pounds of rice to be distributed to the homeless and needy. She also goes to a mountaintop and prays or meditates.

Tran was a little choked up that she will never have her girl, only the boys, but life has taught her that you cannot afford to indulge yourself in getting what you want, but rather you must do what is best for those you are responsible for. She said that therefore, after a week, she will never think about it again and just move on. I got the idea that her way of thinking was how she had made it out of the orphanage, that it was how she had made it to this country, and that it was how she had created her own successful business.

She left saying that she would come back for a checkup and would consider using an IUD (intrauterine device) as her birth-control method. But I do not know if we will see her again unless she has another pregnancy. Her energy seems to go toward the living, and, as she had told me, all but one of her abortions occurred before she was seven weeks pregnant, which for her is not yet life.

I keep thinking that if I had lived her life, I might have her same philosophy.

—Lou

You Never Know

Once again I just counseled a young woman—I will call her Helene—who was shattered by the experience of getting pregnant. She is beautiful, smart, articulate, and a daughter that any parent would be proud of. In high school she took the "chastity pledge" (she would enter into her marriage a virgin) and was a speaker in the national teen impact program that promotes chastity until marriage. It worked until she fell in love.

Then, like many women before her, because she had never thought that she would have sex, Helene was not prepared to protect herself from pregnancy. Overwhelmed with guilt and shame, and not knowing about emergency contraception that can stop a pregnancy before it starts, she did nothing.

The turmoil she described upon finding herself pregnant cannot be imagined, because it went to the core of her identity. Eventually she concluded that abortion was her best choice because it would allow her to maintain her college scholarship and her life goals. Aside from feeling like a hypocrite, she said, the hardest thing for her was that she could not tell her parents, which made her feel like she was being deceitful. She knew that telling them would preclude her from making her own choice about her future and would also let them know that she had violated the pledge. If only parents could see the anguish I see every day in women who have violated this pledge. It is different from the women whose birth-control method failed. Neither woman is happy to be having an abortion, but those who betray this pledge and feel all the judgments associated with it are crushed, and they have a much longer road to self-forgiveness.

It's easy to say, "Well, then she should just not have the abortion," but obviously she had considered that option herself and her decision to discontinue the pregnancy was not one of convenience. Being a contemplative and sensitive young woman, Helene pondered her circumstance deeply, and was forced to confront her smug and false assumption that, of course, adoption was an easy answer to the problem. She kept repeating, "I didn't know it could happen to someone like me."

Maybe it's always easier to decide what others ought to do. Maybe it's always hard to figure out your own life, your own choices. But, having worked in women's health for so long, I know that opinions about abortion change when it happens to you—when it's your life.

My heart breaks for her, but I think that she will be able to forgive herself eventually. She will be forever more tolerant and understanding of others' difficult situations, not just around pregnancy, but in other life issues as well.

These abstinence-only programs that our tax dollars support make me angry. I have been working in this field a long time, and I see women come in to our clinic knowing less and less about how their bodies work, and less about birth-control methods. Young men are abysmally ignorant. It seems to me that we are doing young men and women a disservice by denying them accurate information about their bodies and their sexual health. It's alright to preach the virtues of abstaining from sex, because many young people do begin sexual activity before they are ready for it. But to have taxpayers funding intentional ignorance and depriving the young of information that they need to protect themselves seems worse than naive; it is cruel.

—Lou

Against the Odds

In response to a story we posted on our blog, someone wrote that if we as a society did more for women, there would be less reason for abortion. Well, hallelujah to that idea! Lack of support from existing social systems is the major reason that many, maybe most, women give for terminating their pregnancies. Many of these women are very courageous, coping with problems that many of us have never seen.

Just the other day I talked to a seventeen-year-old—I'll call her Jessica—who was more mature and more thoughtful than many women twice her age. But then, she pretty much has to be. When she was fifteen, her mother threw her out of the house. Jessica, having nowhere else to live, moved in with her boyfriend. She immediately became pregnant, becoming a mother before she turned sixteen. Sadly, her baby was born prematurely, weighing only a bit more than a pound. The baby survived, but she is now a special-needs child—she is blind, has learning disabilities, and has a speech delay.

The stress of the baby's special needs caused Jessica's relationship to break up because, as Jessica said, "We fought all the time. He was working and I was working and going to school. Plus, the baby has to have special intervention therapies four days a week." The baby also gets speech therapy, blindness compensation classes, and pre-Head Start sessions so that she will not fall too far behind her peers since she will forever be a slow learner.

Jessica ended up in a psychiatric hospital when she and her boyfriend broke up because, she says, "I couldn't sleep for nearly a week because of all I had to do." She went into a manic state and had to be medicated in order to calm down enough to sleep. Jessica said that she took the sleeping pills they gave her for a while, but then found she could not keep her appointments with her psychiatrist because she was afraid she would lose her job if she missed any more work. Now she can no longer receive the medication she needs. "Anyhow," she said, "I don't have time to sleep because I want to keep my grades up to go to medical school." Of course, she still has two more years of high school to complete first.

Her mother, thankfully, has taken her back into her house, but is now very angry with her because she wants an abortion. She thinks that Jessica should continue this pregnancy (as does her ex-boyfriend). They are both telling her that she is nothing but a "baby killer." However, they both tell her that they are unable to help her because of their jobs, and both her mom and her ex-boyfriend are going back to school this month as well.

Jessica says that she wavered for over a month about whether to continue the pregnancy, first following their wishes, but then ultimately realizing that she would never be able to create a life for herself and her daughter if she took on one more burden. She said that she has been all alone in this decision, that she has to be the responsible one among the three adults because the others are not. She said, "They can just walk away, and have, so it is up to me to make the right decision for my future."

—Lou

TINY, GOLDEN FEET

LAURI WOLLNER

MY VIEWS ON ABORTION, NOT UNLIKE OTHER TOPICS, HAVE changed over the years. Having been born and raised Catholic, all I ever knew when I was growing up was that having an abortion was a sin. And not just a minor sin, either. It was one that would land me, or anyone I knew, straight in hell. I remember being in high school and attending a meeting in the cafeteria of the small-town school. Other women and girls from the church were there as well. I am not sure what exactly we were doing. I just remember that there were scary photos, according to whoever was leading this event, of what supposedly happens during an abortion and what a fetus looks like. I left there with a tiny pin depicting two little golden feet to stick on my sweater or coat. These feet were to represent how tiny a baby is and they were supposedly life size feet of the average aborted baby. This was also supposed to be a symbol I could wear proudly as a pro-life individual. *Who wouldn't want to be pro-life?* I wondered.

At that time, I believed in everything the church taught me. I was strongly rooted in the pro-life movement. How could anyone justify murder? It all seemed simple enough to me then: Don't have sex, it's a sin. Don't have an abortion, it's a sin. I still had full virgin status and the fear of God in my heart. I was not even *thinking* about sex, much less having it. It was easy to be pro-life then.

Somewhere along the line in college, I began to question more than just the ruling on abortion that a good Catholic had to believe in. I met other people from other states and countries and from all kinds of different religious backgrounds. I began to see the discrepancies in how women and men were treated by the church. I began to see examples of how people used their religion to justify judging others on certain behaviors, and yet not hold themselves to the same standards. They would use the defense that the Bible says A, B, or C, and yet they didn't follow the letter of the law with regard to *everything* the Bible says. It didn't make sense to me that someone could choose what to impose on other people and yet not be consistent on all issues. I wanted to know why a woman couldn't be a priest. I wanted to know why it was a sin to fall in love with someone of the same gender. I wanted to know a lot of things that didn't exactly seem fair. I wondered why the same people who were pro-life and trusted in God to "choose" a woman's pregnancy were the same people who used fertility drugs when they themselves weren't able to become pregnant. And I began to question the church's absolute ruling on abortion. And to wonder if the God I believed in truly had views that were that clear-cut.

And I met women who got pregnant. I met women who got pregnant accidentally. I met women who got pregnant because they wanted to. I met women who got pregnant because they were raped. And I met women who kept their babies, despite their own young age. And I met women who placed their babies for adoption. And I met women who had abortions.

And I heard their stories.

And I heard about the consequences of their decisions, whatever they were.

And I met feminist, pro-choice women.

And I listened to their stories.

And by my senior year of college, I began to change my views on abortion. I began to see why women needed to have the choice about whether to bring a child into her life or not, and that the decision depended on so many different factors. I never stopped wishing that this society could change in ways that would decrease the need for abortion in the first place. But I definitely stopped assuming that it was a clear-cut and simple decision. And I stopped judging the women I knew who had abortions.

I suppose it is worth mentioning here that I lost some of my closest friends from high school around this time. In their opinions, my views had strayed too far from Catholicism. Coming out of the closet and not being a complete heterosexual woman who would marry a man and have children was one reason I lost touch with my friends. But there was one friend in particular, who, I am convinced, was unable to remain friends with me due to my pro-choice views and actions, not my sexuality. She still had one of those pins with the tiny, golden feet from our pro-life days. It saddened me to lose her friendship. To this day, I wonder sometimes if there would ever be a chance of rekindling our friendship, but I assume she is still blindly following what she was taught about "right" and "wrong." I don't feel hostile toward her. I am simply deeply saddened by the loss of her friendship, as she meant a great deal in my life.

When I graduated from college I went on to work in the helping profession. My first job out of college was in a chemical dependency/dual-diagnosis inpatient treatment center. I worked with adult men and women who had been abusing alcohol and drugs and coping with mental illness for the majority of their lives. People abuse substances and their bodies for a number of reasons. Anxiety and an inability to deal with one's emotions is a factor. But one of the key reasons people continue to abuse their bodies is because of some level of self-hatred. Somewhere along the line, they did something that they hate themselves for. And, whether they think their parents won't forgive them, or their God won't forgive them, or whatever, they continue to punish themselves and become their own biggest executioner, and they become unable to let go of whatever has them trapped. I cannot tell you how many of them had unresolved guilt, grief, and/or anger relating to their own abortion or someone close to them having an abortion. I sat with more than one man while he cried because his girlfriend had an abortion. I sat with more than one woman who could not forgive herself for having had one. And, on the flip side, I heard countless horror stories of neglect and abuse of children brought into unhealthy situations in this world.

It was a difficult job. It was a special job. I was in a position to gain the trust of countless individuals who considered themselves "damaged goods," as did the people in their lives. I worked to get them to trust me with their deepest and darkest secrets so that I could help them begin to forgive themselves, something that would have to happen if they had any chance of staying sober and changing their lives. I had to help them explore the religion they were born into and the spirituality they found as adults so that they would have something to believe in and that would make their life worth living again. It was more than an honor and a privilege to be in that position, despite its challenges on any given day. I had to hold my own judgments close to my chest. It would not have been appropriate, professionally or otherwise, to judge these vulnerable individuals. My job was to listen. My job was to ask questions. My job was to help them explore their own beliefs and make decisions on how to save their own lives—not to make decisions for them.

Ironic, then, that I was fired from this job for helping facilitate a client getting an abortion. I can clearly understand, in hindsight, that I had broken a rule of the agency (lending money to a client) and therefore given them a clear-cut reason to terminate my employment. However, it saddens me to return to that time in my memories and know that I was personally against abortion on so many levels and that I ended up losing my job for helping a woman get an abortion. I had heard her stories, though, and I knew about her current circumstances. I knew that she was desperate enough to make the abortion happen with or without my help. I had been given the directive to take her to the clinic once her decision was made and the appointment had been made. In some ways, I was simply doing my job that day and having to struggle in my mind and heart with how it felt to be involved with this abortion. I would not have been able to say, "But wait, I am Catholic, I don't want to do this" without the risk of losing my job. And at that point in my life, I was newly accepting of my pro-choice stance and yet still held hostage, on some level, by the tiny golden feet that had been emblazoned in my heart.

I remained professional and had every intention of ensuring that this client was treated with respect in the process of her ending her pregnancy. How was I to know that the clinic required cash and would not accept checks? What was I supposed to do when the clinic explained to me that she was at the last day of being able to have a "normal" abortion and that she would need to be hospitalized and have surgery if she waited another day? And when they gave us thirty minutes to leave and get cash and come back, what was I supposed to do when she realized her roommate had emptied her bank account? At that moment I made the call to lend her the money. Despite my inner turmoil about abortion, I agreed to lend her the money and take her back to the clinic. To this day, knowing all of the details of her life, what was going on for her, what trauma she had been through, what had occurred for her to be pregnant in the first place—I know I would have no choice but to lend her the money again.

And I know this is hard for pro-lifers to understand, because for them it is all-or-nothing. If they only knew the whole story.

When I lost my job, I began to volunteer at an agency that worked with women who had been raped. It was here that I heard more horror stories of pregnancies that were clearly not wanted. It was here, among other staff and volunteers, that I met some women who were not apologetic about their decision to have an abortion. They had made their decision for countless reasons. And they generally did not have religious guilt attached to their decision.

I have heard too many awful stories of what happened to women before it was legal to have an abortion in this country. I have heard too many stories of the circumstances surrounding conception to say that I am righteous enough to deserve to make that decision for other women. I have heard too many stories about the father who, for one reason or another, is not supportive, or, in some cases, even poses a threat to the potential baby. I have known countless women who were not stable enough emotionally, financially, physically, or spiritually to raise a child.

I have heard too many stories to make that decision for any woman.

Politically, I *have* to be pro-choice.

Black-and-white thinking about something as important as life is not wise.

Imagine if more women talked about their experiences with their families and friends instead of with a counselor or a priest and no one else.

There are staggering numbers of young women who become pregnant without planning to. And there are even more staggering numbers of young men and women who get a sexually transmitted infection, or more than one. Young women and men are told not to have sex. Some are told this in the context of religion. If the current powers in the federal government had their way, the only sex education allowed would be for "abstinence until marriage" education. I understand and appreciate the vulnerability of a young individual when it comes to sexual practices, but what I cannot understand is how people think that telling kids not to have sex actually works. Do they realize that a great number of kids who have been manipulated into accepting "virginity pledges" have begun to have oral and anal sex? They believe they are still virgins, so they think everything is fine. This "just say no" education may allow a young woman to avoid pregnancy, but it certainly won't protect her from, and in many cases it increases her risks for, sexually transmitted infections. Not to mention how much more difficult it will be to avoid sexual intercourse once they begin to engage in other forms of sexual activity.

I wish that we could move toward a society that allows for frank discussions about sexuality. I wish that we could teach the younger generations to protect themselves from any "surprises" after having sex by making well-thought-out decisions regarding what sexual activities they will or will not engage in and when. I wish we could talk honestly and openly with them about how to protect not only their womb and genitals from what can happen when engaging in sexual activities, but also the things that can happen to their self-esteem. I wish we could share our stories of what went well and what went terribly wrong for us as we grew into our sexual selves and that they would be able to hear our stories rather than feel judged and ordered to "behave."

Maybe they would listen, if we actually talked with them.

Maybe we could teach them to have enough knowledge, control over their lives, and self-esteem to make sound choices before they engage in sexual activity.

There are too many complications around sexuality, gender, religion, and politics to have any simple answers that bring us closer to ensuring that we don't have unwanted pregnancies in the first place.

I wish there were no need for abortions.

But there is a need sometimes.

And I believe that my God is much more concerned with the integrity of someone's decision-making and their acceptance of the consequences of those decisions than with the actual decision that they make.

And I believe that neither I, nor any other person, can lay claim to knowing what is right or what is wrong for any woman who is pregnant. She knows best the situation of her life and whether or not her pregnancy is right for her.

I'M NOT SORRY

PANDORA L. LEONG

WHEN I HEARD ABOUT THE "I'M NOT SORRY" WEBSITE (WWW
.imnotsorry.net), I was thrilled. Finally, someone had unapologetically
started a conversation about her abortion and was giving other women a
forum to talk about their abortions without shame. Shame has no place
in my world: I exuberantly purchased an I HAD AN ABORTION T-shirt for
a friend. Half-jokingly, I then made one for her daughter to wear at the
same time that read, "I made the cut."

When I started calling myself a feminist in 1989, when I was eleven
years old, I certainly did not know if I would ever have an abortion, but
I was adamant that I wanted the option available to me. For me, the individual woman is always central to the abortion decision. Potential life
cannot begin to outweigh in importance the impact on the real woman
who's making the choice, whether she faces a fetus that will be born

brain-dead or became pregnant as a result of unprotected sex. Abortion isn't about taking a "life"; it is one situation in which a woman decides that her own life and autonomy are more important to her than the consequence of a particular pregnancy. Abortion currently exists as one decision that a woman can make in a landscape of so many choices that she has no control over: the socio-economic situation of the family she is born into; the "isms" that influence how the world treats her; the fact that she bears the physical burden of reproduction.

The cost of not having choices was evident in the neighborhood where I grew up. Tucked behind a parade of bars and strip joints, my family and others like ours carved out a space between two trailer parks, one street over from the Hells Angels clubhouse. My parents drove me to school because it was not safe to wait at the bus stop. Their behavior seemed paranoid until a classmate was abducted from our bus stop and assaulted. Our friendliest and most affluent neighbor dealt drugs. A prostitute was found dead in a driveway down the street from my house. Suffice it to say, June and Ward wouldn't have let Beaver play in my neighborhood.

Long before my own adolescence, I watched unintended pregnancies govern the range of options women had in my community. Supporting a child meant staying in mediocre or dead-end jobs, or having more than one job; delaying or eliminating chances for higher education; or staying in relationships that were at best unsupportive and at times, abusive. The ability to control one's own reproduction, and the subsequent impact it has on a woman's life, is intimately intertwined with her financial security, or, as was the case in my neighborhood, financial insecurity.

I know all too intimately that people who claim to be "pro-life" care very little about the quality of life real children have, especially poor children. I will start to believe that anti-choice protesters care about women or children outside of the womb when they actually do something constructive, such as lobby for affordable childcare and funding for schools, food stamps, and healthcare for women and children. People who seek to eliminate abortions are too often the same people who object to accurate sex education, emergency contraception, and birth control—all of which could prevent many of the 2.65 million unintended pregnancies each year.[1]

During my teens, my work with women's organizations, clinics, and domestic violence shelters acquainted me with resources that I knew might one day be crucial to a neighbor or a friend. And it got me out of my neighborhood. Frankly, the struggle for reproductive autonomy was just one of the many challenges facing women in my community, but it was one that seemed less overwhelming than the snarled knot of multiple oppressions entangling the lives of those around me.

In the thirty-three years since *Roe v. Wade*, the reproductive health movement that gave me a political home and taught me to be a feminist activist has been withering away. Polls indicate that fewer women my age identify as pro-choice than did in my mother's generation. More than 550 hospitals and individual practitioners stopped providing abortions between 1992 and 2000, a decrease of 24 percent.[2] During the 2005 legislative session alone, twenty states enacted twenty-seven laws designed to restrict access to abortion and reproductive health. The uncompromised feminist slogan "free abortion on demand" has been replaced by the kinder, gentler "safe, legal, and rare."

I am clearly outside the mainstream of public opinion about social issues in the United States; but within the pro-choice movement itself, I also struggle with issues that rarely get aired, even inside our camp. At the risk of inciting the wrath of people I have marched with, worked for, and slept with (don't worry, those are three separate groups), I confess to opinions that may sow more discontent than do my attempts at fashion.

At the March for Women's Lives in 2004, I wound my way around the National Mall with a group of high school students from New York City.

As our cluster of people of color marched our way through the masses of mostly white women, three questions preoccupied me: "Is this demonstration going to affect the election?" "Will everyone make it back to the bus?" and mostly "When is this movement going to look like me?"

I have waited over fifteen years for the answer to the last question. In my work as a feminist activist, I'm typically one of the very few brown faces at demonstrations and meetings about abortion rights or breast cancer or domestic violence. It's not that these issues don't affect communities of color: The concurrent effects of racism and poverty usually mean they affect us more; however, we are usually too busy dealing with other issues that influence us just as much or more—so many things that those who are more advantaged cannot begin to imagine. From racial profiling to making enough money to put food on the table, the daily struggle for survival often monopolizes our energy.

The majority of the signs at the march were testament to the lack of understanding about the multiplicity of issues for women who share a belief in reproductive autonomy. The predominant slogans—"It's Your Choice, Not Theirs," "Stand Up For Choice," "Keep Abortion Legal"—disregarded the fact that not everyone has the same array of "choices" available, and that legal abortion does not necessarily mean accessible abortion. Having ignored the women at the margins, it's not surprising that what's left of the pro-choice movement is in crisis.

This one-size-fits-all feminism on display at the March for Women's Lives hurts the movement overall and shortchanges the most vulnerable women in our society. All too often, many low-income women and women of color are in positions where we cannot exercise our legal rights: just three years after *Roe v. Wade* was decided, Congress approved the Hyde Amendment, which prohibits funding for abortion for poor women and women in the military. We know Roe's name, but how many people know the story of Rosie Jimenez, who died from an illegal abortion a year after Hyde passed because she couldn't afford a legal, safe abortion? Thirty-four states require parental involvement in a minor's decision to have an abortion. Twenty-four states have mandatory waiting periods that place a huge burden on the women who live in the 86 percent of counties that have no abortion provider and who must travel—sometimes to another state—for treatment. Abortion restrictions are racist and classist in their application.

The reproductive rights movement has ceded too much ground. Six in ten women who had abortions in 2002 were already mothers. If they lived in one of the many states with a waiting period, they would have needed additional childcare, which can be a prohibitive cost especially when combined with the cost of transportation and possible housing. In most of the country, we are defending a right that only adult women who have enough money to pay for both the abortion procedure and childcare and who live in urban areas—can access.

Recent attempts by anti-choice legislators to establish fetal personhood in the legal realm actively harms women who already face considerable odds. Pregnant women with drug and alcohol problems, or who cannot afford to get prenatal care, have been routinely charged and incarcerated under state versions of the Unborn Victims of Violence Act, which criminalizes actions against a fetus rather than increasing penalties for violence against women.[3] These prosecutions pose the greatest threat to women who wish to carry their babies to term and raise them, because they scare the women away from prenatal care and deny them access to drug treatment. When courts intervene to charge pregnant women for using alcohol and/or illegal drugs while pregnant or for refusing medical treatment, it is most often women of color and low-income women who are charged.

A more inclusive pro-choice movement must include a broader array of social issues in its platform. Accurate education about sexuality, affordable health insurance, and economic options that make it possible to support the children that women may want to have or already have are all part of a more comprehensive reproductive justice agenda. Reproductive autonomy should encompass some degree of *freedom to* have healthy children in a safe environment as well as *freedom from* an unwanted pregnancy.

That said, I am reluctant to extend uncompromised access to reproductive technology. These days, conception occurs in test tubes, embryos are selected through genetic testing, and women well past menopause can give birth. For the last thirty years, women of privilege have embraced the language of "choice" when it comes to accessing reproductive technologies while watching conservatives chip away at the reproductive rights of their less advantaged sisters. It can cost as much as $35,000 for each attempted round of in vitro fertilization (IVF). In a country of glaring economic disparities, the money spent enabling women of means to bear the children they choose could instead be spent feeding the one in five black and Latino children who go to school hungry.[4] Why do we need to create more children instead of caring for those who are already here?

As someone with a history of personal and professional commitment to both the reproductive rights movement and the queer community, I was heartened to see the Causes in Common campaign, launched by the LGBT Community Center in New York City, to reach out to the reproductive justice community. These movements both grow out of a philosophy of sexual autonomy and share interests ranging from sex education to freedom from violence. However, at the risk of never finding another woman willing to sleep with me, I must say I was baffled to see "access to reproductive technologies for all people" in the Statement of Principles. My reflexive thought: *What? I didn't sign up for IVF and surrogates for everyone!* Lesbians and gay men seeking to have children should not face discrimination when accessing these technologies but, in a country where forty-five million people do not have health insurance and another sixteen million are underinsured, one marvels at the notion that insurance companies are paying for these enhancement technologies. I am not comfortable with only the wealthy having the ability to afford assisted reproductive technologies, but I would rather see precious healthcare dollars spent on people who already exist. Infertility—whether due to age or the sex of your partner—is not a medical condition in my book; it's an opportunity cost. IVF is a luxury, especially in a world where one billion people globally lack basic healthcare.

Reproductive technologies that rely on harvesting eggs or surrogacy also invite the commodification and commercialization of women's bodies. By and large, the women who can afford to pay for these treatments enjoy the benefits of a very different socioeconomic position than women who are tempted to "donate" their eggs for compensation or agree to surrogacy. Australia, Canada, and much of Europe recognize this risk; Canada has made it a felony to financially (or otherwise) compensate egg donors.

In fact, a new technology has challenged my belief that a woman should have the right to have an abortion for any reason of her choosing: A company called Acu-Gen Biolab started selling Baby Gender Mentor, a test that claims to be able to detect the sex of a fetus as early as the fifth week of pregnancy. Sex-selection technology has long been couching sales pitches in the language of consumerism. MicroSort, another company marketing sex-selection technology, has an advertisement asking, "Do you want to choose the gender of your next baby?"[5] What this advertisement fails to articulate is that early sex testing provides couples the option of choosing to abort on the basis of sex.

As a movement, we need to have a social debate about the merits of abortion for sex selection in a world that not only privileges but "chooses" male babies. While many couples in the United States use sex-selection technologies to add a daughter to a family that already has at least one son, the preference for male children is clearly alive and well domestically and abroad. Reproductive technologies not only commodify women as incubators, but they disproportionately affect different communities. China's one-child policy, combined with a cultural preference for boys, has led to as many as forty million abortions and infanticides.[6] In India, figures indicate that upward of ten million female fetuses have been aborted over the past twenty years.[7] In the United States, women are not obligated to give their rationale for aborting, but what is known is that couples having a female child are 5 percent more likely to divorce than couples expecting or raising a male child; for unmarried couples expecting a child, couples expecting a boy are more likely to get married. The preference for males grows more pronounced as couples have more daughters: Parents with three girls are almost 10 percent more likely to divorce than parents of three boys.[8] Combined, this research suggests that there is indeed a cross-cultural preference for boys. It is irresponsible to promote sex selection without acknowledging the misogyny still rampant throughout our world and with no thought for what that could mean to future generations.

Sex selection is the first step into the world of genetic selection. We already have tests for a range of genetic anomalies such as Down syndrome and cystic fibrosis. The mapping of the human genome raises larger questions about abortion and genetics: Should a woman abort a fetus if she finds out it may be susceptible to breast cancer? If a homosexual gene is found? If research suggests a genetic link to violence? As a movement, we must think strategically about our relationship to reproductive technologies and the disparities within and exacerbated by them.

Riding the El in Chicago recently, I looked up to see a poster that proclaimed, WOMEN DESERVE BETTER. Heartened to see a feminist sentiment advertised in public transit, I leaned forward to read the fine print. It was an anti-abortion ad.

Women *do* deserve better. We deserve safe, affordable contraception and broad sex education in schools. We deserve to decide when and if we have children and we deserve to be able to raise our children in a safe environment. We deserve to be able to access abortion services at our local hospital or provider's office without her or him needing to wear a bulletproof vest. We deserve to live free from violence in our streets and in our homes and at the hands of those who are supposed to protect us. We deserve affordable childcare, healthcare, and public education that adequately prepares students for higher education or to learn an occupational trade. We deserve jobs that pay living wages. I started volunteering at women's organizations because all women deserve not just "choice" in bodily integrity, but better choices throughout their lives.

Underlying any choice is the question: *"Who* has the choice?" To what extent do all women get to access the full array of options? What do these decisions mean for individual women and for their lives? For me, growing up working-class vividly demonstrated the importance of social justice and economic equality. Consequently, reproductive justice is representative of more than just the choices a woman has when she can already afford a place to live, food to eat, and healthcare. Reproductive rights are just some of the issues feminists of color mobilize around; we're trying to create a world based on social justice.

I no longer wear my T-shirt that claims, I AM THE FACE OF PRO-CHOICE AMERICA because I know *I* am not (unless it's a photo op). But I am proud to be a part of the reproductive justice movement in the United States. I'm not sorry that I have worked and continue to work with so many wonderful women, even if the vast majority of them are middle-class and white. I am sorry that more of us with fewer privileges do not feel welcome or able to participate in this movement. I am proud of the work I do daily that keeps abortion within reach for all women and girls—regardless of class. I feel fortunate to have a job that allows me the joy of helping women carry out a range of decisions that affirm the importance of their lives. In the long term, my hope is that this can ensure that more of their daughters and sons "make the cut." The struggle for reproductive justice speaks to principles that are core to my identity as a feminist. Our work now is to continue cultivating a movement that supports the issues and needs of all women.

MIFEPRISTONE

LAURA FRASER

WHEN EMILY MULHERAN WAS IN HER EARLY TWENTIES, SHE STARTED
hearing voices. They filled her head with comments about everything
she saw or did, and yelled at her to hurt herself. Mulheran, who has
been diagnosed with psychotic depression, also had tactile hallucinations, imagining that someone was constantly pricking her. Twice, while
very depressed, she followed the voices that told her to kill herself, over-
dosing on over-the-counter and prescription drugs. She barely survived.

When she is not in the throes of her mental illness, Mulheran, now
thirty-four, is a successful web designer. She has been hospitalized for her
illness and has taken many kinds of medications, most of which haven't
worked. It wasn't until a year ago, when she was doing research on the
Internet about her condition, that she came across a clinical trial for a
new drug that she says saved her life: mifepristone. "I was literally at the

end of my rope," she says. "Mifepristone made all my symptoms—the delusions and hallucinations—go away. It's like a miracle drug."

Few people know mifepristone as a promising anti-psychotic drug. Instead, mifepristone, also called RU-486, is more commonly known as the "abortion pill," approved by the FDA in September 2000 for use in ending unwanted pregnancies of up to seven weeks. But researchers say the drug is the first in a class of new drugs that may be used to treat a number of other conditions, including fibroids, endometriosis, depression, breast cancer, a hormonal disease called Cushing's syndrome, and a type of brain tumor called meningioma. Currently, the drug is undergoing clinical trials for several of these uses, but it's a long way from FDA approval. Outside of these trials, the drug has been dispensed to only seventy-one patients who have life-threatening illnesses under the Mifepristone Compassionate Use Program directed by the Feminist Majority Foundation, a nonprofit organization. Scientists worry that if the drug is banned for use as an abortifacient (a medication that induces an abortion) research on its other, unrelated uses may grind to a halt.

Over the past decade, mifepristone has been embroiled in political controversy. Given the current political climate, with two new conservative Supreme Court justices on the bench, and abortion rights being chipped away with nearly every new ruling, mifepristone is bound to come under even greater scrutiny. Mifepristone causes a medical abortion in early pregnancy, and at one point pro-choice feminists hoped that it would diffuse the debate that surrounded surgical abortions. If any doctor could prescribe the pill, then the harassment and terrorism practiced by anti-choice protesters at abortion clinics would be rendered obsolete. But groups that oppose abortion have ascertained that abortion will never be as easy as a quick trip to the doctor for a prescription (mifepristone actually would never be that easy; it requires several trips—one for the mifepristone itself, one to get a prescription for an accompanying pill that speeds along the process, and one for an essential follow-up visit). Anti-choice opposition to mifepristone has ensured that the drug will not only be an unfeasible alternative for terminating early pregnancies, but that it will not reach the market to treat a wide variety of medical conditions, including ones that may be life-threatening.

Approved in twenty-nine countries and used by more than one million women worldwide, mifepristone's introduction to the United States was slowed when anti-abortion groups denounced it as a "human pesticide" and a "death pill." To prevent it from being introduced to the United States, they used boycotts to pressure the French and German companies that manufactured the drug. Pro-choice groups—which point out that since mifepristone only works very early in pregnancy, it actually prevents late-term abortions, such as those recently banned under the so-called Partial-Birth Abortion Ban Act—negotiated with the companies to bring the drug to the United States during the Clinton administration when it gained FDA approval. However, the terms of distribution were so limited—the drug is only accessible to physicians who already perform surgical abortions—that it could not live up to its promise to taking abortion procedures from the highly identifiable, targetable, and potentially violent margins of abortion clinics into mainstream medicine. Now the drug is distributed by Danco Laboratories, a private company, under strict FDA guidelines: It can't be prescribed by just any doctor or picked up at a pharmacy, like most drugs; it can only be given directly to patients by physicians who already perform surgical abortions and follow a strict regimen for its use. Since mifepristone was approved in the United States, over 200,000 American women have taken the drug to end early pregnancies.

Recently, the drug was attacked again after a California teenager died of septic shock after taking mifepristone (and emergency room personnel, apparently unaware she'd had a medical miscarriage, gave her painkillers and sent her home). Several politicians promptly called upon

Congress to suspend the drug and review its FDA approval. "If there is an error, you ground the fleet and investigate the safety problems," says John Hart, spokesperson for Representative Jim DeMint (R-S.C.), who introduced a bill to ban the drug.

The legislation is one more in a string of political efforts to ban a drug because it induces abortion. The FDA has found, through its regular research channels, that the drug is safe and effective. It has been targeted not because of its uncertain medical record, or its risks, but because of a larger effort by the Bush administration and Congress to replace legitimate science with right-wing ideology. In a climate where even the "morning after" pill (a high-dose of hormones taken within 72 hours of sexual intercourse in order to prevent pregnancy) is being derided as an abortifacient, it is unlikely that there will be funds to research mifepristone's effectiveness in achieving the same controversial outcome. Scientists, afraid of getting funds cut, are reluctant to pursue studies on a drug that has become a political hot potato.

While those who would ban the drug say it was hurried through FDA approval, Heather O'Neill, a spokesperson for Danco, says that the safety of mifepristone—brand name Mifeprex—is well established. "Mifeprex underwent rigorous testing and review before being approved," she says. The drug, taken along with another drug, misoprostol, two days later to induce uterine contractions, is 92–95 percent effective, and is now used in about 8 percent of U.S. abortions—a percentage that is rising rapidly as more women learn about it as an option. O'Neill says there have been only two deaths associated with the drug in the United States; one due to a burst ectopic pregnancy (a labeled contraindication that physicians are supposed to screen out), and the other, the California death, due to infection. "Childbirth or any kind of abortion or miscarriage can create conditions that can result in infection," O'Neill says. "There is no medical evidence that Mifeprex presents a special risk of infection." To put the Mifeprex deaths in perspective, there are thirteen pregnancy-related deaths per 100,000 live births in the United States; taking the drug is much safer than carrying a pregnancy to term. Other drugs have much worse track records: Viagra, according to the *Journal of the American Medical Association*, has caused 564 deaths in sixteen million users as of 1999.

Whatever the result of the proposed ban on using mifepristone for abortion, researchers who are studying the drug for other uses say that the political situation has made it much more difficult to study the drug, and a ban would certainly make the situation worse. Dr. Steve Eisinger, a University of Rochester OB/GYN who has done clinical trials using mifepristone to treat uterine fibroids, worries that politics may get in the way of a promising drug. "This is a very interesting drug that has many potential important uses completely unrelated to abortion," he says. "It would be a crying shame if politically motivated efforts were made to prevent this drug from getting to the American public."

John Hart, Representative DeMint's spokesperson, says the ban on mifepristone would only affect its use as an abortifacient, not its other potential uses. But if it were banned here as an abortifacient, that would make it difficult, if not impossible, for researchers to obtain the drug. Unlike other pharmaceutical companies, which sell a number of drugs, Danco, which supplies mifepristone for clinical trials in the United States at cost, has only one product—mifepristone. If it were banned, Danco would likely go out of business and mifepristone wouldn't be available anywhere.

Already the political climate has discouraged researchers who are interested in the drug. "Because of political difficulties, many researchers have troubles getting supplies and funding for the drug, so they jump ship and study something else," says Dr. Beth Jordan, director of the Feminist Majority Foundation's Compassionate Use Program. "Taking it off the market would prevent leading scientists from conducting further research for life-threatening conditions."

The reason researchers are so interested in mifepristone is that it's a breakthrough drug. It's the first in a whole new class of drugs—called SPRMS, or selective progesterone receptor modulators—that can treat diseases related to the female hormone progesterone. Mifepristone works by blocking the female hormone progesterone, fitting like a key in a lock into the progesterone receptors and preventing the progesterone from coming in. In its use as an abortion pill, mifepristone causes a miscarriage because progesterone is essential for continuing a pregnancy. Without progesterone, the lining of the uterus breaks down and the fertilized egg is expelled. Used early enough as a contraceptive, it prevents a fertilized egg from being implanted into the uterine wall.

Mifepristone is being used in low doses as emergency contraception in China and Great Britain. Dr. Eric Schaff, a professor of obstetrics and gynecology at the University of Rochester who heads a team of physicians conducting several studies with mifepristone, says the advantage of the drug as an emergency contraceptive is that it has no side effects. By blocking progesterone, the drug puts women in the same state they're in for the first two weeks of their menstrual cycle, when they naturally make no progesterone. "Women typically feel fine," says Schaff, "and it's very safe." Other studies have shown that at low doses, mifepristone would be an effective once-a-month birth control pill.

Mifepristone shows promise in treating other conditions that are fed by the hormone progesterone. The drug has been effective in shrinking fibroid tumors in the uterus, which depend on progesterone to grow. In a year-long study of twenty women, Dr. Eisinger found that mifepristone typically shrank fibroid tumors by half. Fibroids affect 40–70 percent of American women, though most are too small to be symptomatic. When fibroids get large they cause very heavy periods, often resulting in anemia and severe pain as they press on nearby organs. Fibroids contain both estrogen and progesterone receptors, but anti-estrogen drugs cause side effects such as hot flashes and bone loss, so the anti-progesterone drug may be more promising. Most women with large fibroids need to have hysterectomies, but Eisinger says mifepristone may shrink fibroids to the degree that women could avoid surgery. He says that in low doses, the women had few side effects. "Women taking this medication felt really, really good."

Priscilla Putnam, a fifty-one-year-old school administrator, participated in the clinical study. She had a large fibroid and experienced heavy menstrual periods, back pain, frequent urination, and bloating. She took the drug for a year. "The results were amazing," she says. "The fibroid shrank, and I felt so much better." When the study was over, she went off the medication and the fibroids grew back. She's disappointed that she can't get the drug, but understands that the FDA needs more studies and data on long-term use to approve it as safe for treating fibroids. But she's worried that the political atmosphere might slow that process. "I'm concerned that this medical treatment, that offers relief for women who have large fibroids, will get mixed in with the whole anti-abortion movement. They're two separate issues." Under the terms of the Compassionate Use Program, Putnam and others with fibroids can't get mifepristone because the FDA doesn't consider fibroids a life-threatening condition.

Mifepristone has also helped people who have a type of brain tumor called meningioma, which has progesterone receptors. Doris Laird, a retired professor in Tallahassee, Florida, has been taking mifepristone for her meningioma tumor for ten years under the Compassionate Use Program. "It has saved my life and my sight three times," she says. Prior to using the drug, she'd had three twenty-four-hour surgeries for the tumor, which had caused blinding headaches and wrapped itself around her optic nerve, threatening her sight. Since she's been on the drug, CT scans reveal that the tumor has stopped growing.

The drug may also be useful in treating uterine cancer. As with other conditions, the treatment is related to the progesterone receptors in the cells. In lab studies, Dr. Lois Ramondetta, a gynecologic oncologist at the

M.D. Anderson Cancer Center at the University of Texas, found that mifepristone was effective in arresting the growth of cancer cells that had progesterone receptors. In a clinical trial with patients who have recurrent and late-stage endometrial cancer, Ramondetta has seen some evidence that mifepristone can help stabilize a disease that is usually, at that point, incurable. Her studies have also shown that mifepristone reacts differently to different types of progesterone receptors, of which there are many. Like tamoxifen, which is an anti-estrogen drug that blocks estrogen in the breasts but stimulates another type of estrogen receptor in the endometrium, mifepristone has the paradoxical effect of stimulating progesterone in the endometrium, which slows the growth of cancer cells. "We're learning a lot about progesterone receptors, but it's very early," Ramondetta says. Mifepristone has opened the door to studying a number of different ways progesterone works. "Once we learn a little more, we should make some big differences."

Mifepristone has another property that makes it very interesting to scientists: It is an antiglucocortisoid, meaning that it blocks the stress hormone cortisol. In fact, the drug was originally developed in France for use as an anti-cortisol drug, not as an abortion pill. Having too much cortisol is related to depression, alcoholism, anorexia, other nervous system disorders, as well as Cushing's syndrome. A National Institutes of Health study showed that the drug helped patients who were gravely ill with Cushing's syndrome, a disease that affects ten to fifteen of every million people and results in severe fatigue, depression, thin skin, upper-body obesity, and other debilitating symptoms. In the study, more than 50 percent of patients using the drug found it controlled or reversed the effects of the disease. Currently, several patients with Cushing's syndrome are being treated under the Compassionate Use Program.

There are several studies in the works that are using mifepristone to treat severe depression. Many people with severe depression and psychosis (having delusions and hallucinations) have high levels of cortisol, so a drug that blocks cortisol can bring them relief. In two Stanford University studies, patients with psychotic major depression who took the drug showed "significant reductions" in their psychosis in less than a week, leading Stanford psychiatrist Alan Schatzberg to speculate that the drug might open up new methods for treating the illness that are more acceptable than the current standard: electroshock therapy. Other, smaller studies have shown that patients with obsessive compulsive disorder, manic depression, and other mental illnesses may benefit from the drug.

Still, for any of these uses, FDA approval is far away. "All of them would require much more research before being submitted to the FDA," says Danco spokesperson O'Neill. "It's a useful beginning, but only a beginning."

Patients like Emily Mulheran hope the drug is approved soon. After the clinical trials with mifepristone ended, the effects of the drug lasted six months before she began to have delusions again. Desperate for the drug, she tried getting it from a Planned Parenthood clinic, which was not licensed to give it to her for that use. She ended up opting for electroshock therapy, which was ineffective and caused complications, including memory loss and symptoms that affected her ability to function at work. She's now trying to get mifepristone through the Compassionate Use Program. "It's been very frustrating, and I'm praying that the drug will be approved," she says. Meanwhile, she has emailed her representatives and President Bush to oppose the proposed ban on the drug. "Mifepristone is not just an abortion drug," she says. "Before people take the drastic step to ban it, they should understand this is a drug that's going to help countless people's lives."

IS THERE LIFE AFTER *ROE?*
How to Think About the Fetus
FRANCES KISSLING

IN THE THIRTY YEARS SINCE *ROE V. WADE* USHERED IN A NEW PARA-
digm in the legal understanding of the right to choose abortion, there
has been little about the issue that has not been said—and said time
and time again. Supporters of choice have argued that it is important to
recognize women as autonomous persons with the moral capacity and
moral right to decide whether a pregnancy will be aborted or brought to
term. We have enhanced our core argument with references to broader
values such as religious freedom, opposition to government intervention
in our personal lives, and the right to medical privacy. The most powerful of pro-choice messages has been the multifaceted question, "Who
decides?" which highlights both women's rights and the importance of
keeping government out of the bedroom without ever mentioning either.
Inherent in our focus on women's rights has been our belief that fetal

life does not attain, at any point in pregnancy, a value that is equivalent to that of born persons, specifically women, infants, or children, who are most often cited in discussions of abortion. Our belief about what value fetal life may possess is not yet well articulated, and pro-choice supporters are not of one mind on this question. Neither, it should be noted, are the world's religions, ethicists, or theologians.

Those who are opposed to legal abortion seem more certain and monolithic on the question of the value of fetal life. Their core message has been simple: Fetal life at all stages of development has an inviolable right to life. Fetuses are, they claim, the most vulnerable persons among us and our humanity requires that we protect them from destruction by intentional abortion. This position did not resonate with most Americans at the time *Roe* was decided and it still has little support. In fact, in 1973, public opinion largely favored legal abortion and people spent little if any time thinking about the fetus. We were, after all, in the midst of a sexual and reproductive revolution brought on by the discovery of the Pill and an increasing acceptance of women's rights. The tragedy of women dying or suffering serious health consequences following illegal abortion was front and center. Added to this was the strong desire, felt by many couples, to have fewer children, which was seen as central to achieving the working-class dream of owning your own home, sending your kids to a good college, and having more meaningful and better-paid work.

For both supporters and opponents of abortion rights, single-focus positions have presented some difficulties. Supporters of abortion rights are pushed to the limits on abortions later in pregnancy and on the question of the extent to which abortion can be regulated, if not restricted. Those who oppose abortion rights have struggled with the logical conclusion of the claim that there is no distinction in fetal value at any stage in pregnancy and have ended up opposing abortion in tragic cases, such as after rape and for very young women who have been victims of incest.

Consistency (and here the phrase, "A foolish consistency is the hobgoblin of little minds," comes to mind) has meant that they have had to oppose embryonic stem-cell research that could contribute to saving lives and emergency contraception for women who have been raped on the slight chance that a conception may have already taken place.

After a number of failed attempts to overturn *Roe* outright, opponents of abortion developed a long-term incremental legislative strategy designed as much to win the hearts and minds of moderate supporters of abortion rights as to change the law itself. They aimed to chip away at access to abortion services for groups perceived to be powerless and unpopular, such as poor women and adolescents. In the case of poor women, they claimed they did not want their tax dollars to pay for a service they considered immoral. In the case of adolescents, they asserted that no adolescent should be treated without the consent of her parents. However, their major goal was to convince people that fetuses are indeed persons. In recent years, anti-choice activists have poured resources into ensuring that the law treat fetuses as persons and highlighting scientific advances in fetal medicine. In spite of the anti-abortion movement's incremental strategy, its leaders are clear that their ultimate goal is an absolute ban on all abortions except those needed as immediate lifesaving measures. This obstinate insistence on an absolute legal ban is the major obstacle to what might have been the development of an abortion praxis that combined respect for the fundamental right of women to choose abortion with an ethical discourse that included the exploration of how other values might also be respected, including the value of developing human life.

Instead, those committed to the right to choose have felt forced to defend what appears to be an absolute right to abortion that brooks no consideration of other values—legal or moral. This often means a reluctance to even consider whether or not fetal life has value, or an attempt to define that value or to see how it can be promoted without restricting access to legal abortion. As the fetus has become more visible through both anti-abortion efforts and advances in fetal medicine, this stance has become less satisfying as either a moral framework or a message strategy that responds to the concerns of many Americans who are generally both supportive of and uncomfortable with legal abortion.

RIGHTS AND VALUES

I believe women have a basic human right to decide what to do about a pregnancy. Other well-established human rights concepts bolster this argument, including bodily integrity, the right to health, the right to practice one's religion (or not), and the right to be free from religious laws in modern democratic societies. Despite the assertions of some very intelligent pro-lifers that the abortion issue is a question of the human rights of the fetus, the human rights community is moving steadily toward recognizing a woman's right to choose, and there is no countervailing view in this community that even considers the question of whether or not fetuses are rights-bearing entities.

But the abortion issue is not one in which only rights are at stake. There are at least three central values that need to be part of the public conversation about abortion and, as appropriate, influence behavior, if not law. They are:

1. The human right of women to decide whether or not to continue a pregnancy.

2. A respect for human life that takes the form of what Daniel Callahan called more than thirty years ago "a moral presumption in favor of life."

3. A commitment to ensure that provisions which permit the taking of life (whether it be fetal, animal, or plant) not coarsen

the overall fabric of society and our attitudes toward each other as well as toward developing human life.

First, and I would say most important, is our obligation to respect in law and social thought the right of women to bodily autonomy. Generally speaking, no woman should be forced to carry a pregnancy to term without her consent. I am revolted by the thought that a law banning most or all abortions would, if it were to be more than a rhetorical exercise, require an enforcement mechanism that actively forces women to continue pregnancies that they believe to be antithetical to their needs or identities. But the right to choose abortion is not absolute, and in practice and law, even those of us most ardently pro-choice do not demand absolutism. The law clearly does not recognize that the right is so fundamental that it requires the government to provide abortion services routinely for free. The first restriction of *Roe* was the court decision that freed the federal government from the obligation to provide funding for abortions for women dependent on the government for their medical care. Medical ethics, on the other hand, demands that a patient who arrives at a health service at death's door must be treated even if he or she has no money. Our clinics turn away some women who cannot afford abortions. We insist on full payment in advance, sometimes delaying an abortion until the pregnancy is further advanced and carrying a greater risk of complications.

Many accept that post-viability abortions can be denied unless the woman's life is at risk, the fetus has a condition that is truly incompatible with life, or there is a serious health risk to the woman. We are thus prepared to "force," or at least not to facilitate, an abortion at eight months for a woman who is, for example, abandoned by her partner and no longer wishes to have a child. But, with those limits acknowledged, we believe a good society will make it possible for women who do not want to be pregnant to get safe, dignified, and compassionate abortion services. It will also do everything it can to help women and men prevent pregnancies if they do not want to have children. This is not necessarily out of respect for the fetus, but out of respect for women. The act of taking life in abortion is defensible and can have positive results, but in and of itself is not a moral good. We should do everything we can to enable people to live lives that affirm human beings and other forms of life that are not harmful to our world. One colleague who reviewed this article noted that the term "right to life" and its unrelenting and vague formulation obscures the fact that some life is dangerous and does not deserve to be respected. Cancer cells are a form of life, as are viruses like polio and HIV/AIDS. Should they be respected?

VALUING FETAL LIFE

This brings us to the second value of a good society: respect for life, including fetal life. Why should we allow this value to be owned by those opposed to abortion? Are we not capable of walking and chewing gum at the same time; of valuing life and respecting women's rights? Have we not ceded too much territory to anti-abortion forces by not articulating the value of fetal life? In an important op-ed in *The New York Times*, author William Saletan claimed that "supporters of abortion rights . . . still don't know how to articulate the value of unborn human life." Saletan makes a good point, but he does not pursue it and offers no suggestions for how we might articulate this value.

Such an effort will take a lot of work and involve exposing deep differences among supporters of choice regarding our views on the inherent value of fetal life on its own terms and in relation to women's rights. An interesting thought exercise might help to clarify what pro-choice (and anti-abortion) leaders believe about fetal value. Imagine a world in which it were possible to remove fetuses prior to viability from women's bodies and allow them to develop in a non-uterine environment. Perhaps they could be implanted in men or other women who want them; perhaps they could develop in a specially equipped nursery. In this world, medicine is so far advanced that this could be accomplished painlessly and without risking the health of either the woman or the fetus. Of course, this is at present largely a fantasy, and by the time we can make it real, we will no doubt have found the ideal, risk-free, failure-free contraceptive; but let's pretend.

What are the first five concerns and reactions that come to your mind? Is one of them the fact that this would mean fetuses need not die? My own experience in presenting this option to both advocates and opponents of abortion is that the fetus's life is rarely a consideration. Among the most interesting reactions of those who are pro-choice is a concern that some women might find the continued existence of the fetus painful for them, or that women have a right to ensure that their genetic material does not enter the world. Abortion in this sense becomes the guarantee of a dead fetus, if desired, rather than the removal of the fetus from an unwilling host, the woman. To even offer women such an option is, some think, cruel. For some, the right to choose abortion seems to include the right to be protected from thinking about the fetus and from any pain that might result from others talking about the fetus in value-laden terms. In this construct, it is hard to identify any value fetal life might have.

This level of sensitivity to protecting women from their feelings takes other forms. For example, some pro-choice advocates have objected to public discussion of abortion that includes concern for the number of abortions that occur in the United States, or that has as its goal reducing the number of abortions. Some bristled at President Clinton's formula that abortion should be "safe, legal, and rare." If abortion is justifiable, why should it be rare? Even the suggestion that abortion is a moral matter as well as a legal one has caused concern that such a statement might make women feel guilty. Words like "baby" are avoided, not just because they are inaccurate, but because they are loaded.

In a society where women have long been victims of moral

discourse, these concerns are somewhat understandable, but they do not contribute much toward convincing people that when pro-choice advocates say they value fetal life, it is more than lip service.

The reaction of the anti-abortion side to the idea that a fetus could be removed from the body of an unwilling woman is equally troubling. Again, one rarely hears cries of joy that fetal lives would be saved. The focus also is on the woman. But here, the view that women are, by their nature, made for childbearing dominates. Women have an obligation to continue pregnancies, to suffer the consequences of their sexuality. It is unnatural to even think that fetuses could become healthy and happy people if they did not spend nine months in the womb of a woman. One is led to believe that, for those opposed to abortion, it is not saving fetuses that matters, but preserving a social construct in which women breed.

THINKING ABOUT MESSAGES

Thought exercises clearly have their limits, and there is much that could be done to balance women's rights with an expression of fetal value without resorting to science fiction. A first step might be a conversation among pro-choice leaders that explored what we think about the value of fetal life. You cannot talk cogently about things you have not thought about or discussed. And not thinking leads to mistakes. At times there is a kind of pro-choice triumphalism in operation. Abortion is a serious matter; it is a woman's right, and no woman needs to apologize for making this decision. On the other hand, no woman needs to brag about her choice, and the decision of one pro-choice organization to sell T-shirts announcing I HAD AN ABORTION was in poor taste and diminished the seriousness of the act of abortion.

A second step might include care not to confuse legal arguments with moral messages. Too often the legal arguments that win in a court of law are the very arguments that lose in the court of public opinion. Anti-abortion legislators have played on this tendency by introducing legislation that appears unrelated to abortion, that "protects" the fetus. The most emotionally charged legislation was the Unborn Victims of Violence Act, which introduced an extra penalty for anyone convicted of harming a fetus during the commission of certain federal crimes (separate from penalties related to the injury or death of the pregnant woman). It gave separate legal status to a fertilized egg, embryo, or fetus, even if the woman did not know she was pregnant. Crafted in the wake of the deaths of Laci and Conner Peterson, the legislation captured people's sympathy. Pro-choice responses that focused on the fact that the legislation was not needed, or that argued that it was a backdoor attempt to eviscerate the right to abortion, made us seem heartless. As difficult as it may be, this might have been one piece of legislation we could have tolerated. In the war of ideas, not every hill is worth climbing.

Until now, the conventional wisdom in the pro-choice movement has been that talking about fetal life is counterproductive. In the polarized climate created by absolutists opposed to legal abortion, a siege mentality has developed. Pro-choice advocates fear that any discussion of fetal value will strengthen the claim that if the fetus has value, abortion must be prohibited in all or most circumstances.

In addition to the fear that acknowledging fetal life as valuable would lead to making abortion illegal is the reality that the ethical discussion about when the fetus becomes a person—whether theological, legal, sociological, or medical—seems abstract to most people. In theology, the question has traditionally focused on when it is most likely that God gives the developing fetus a soul, a discourse pretty much abandoned by both traditional and innovative theologians; in sociology, most often the capacity for relationships is central—the issue is when one can say a meaningful relationship exists between the fetus and society; in medicine, the weight is on viability and on the physical and mental capacity of the fetus—when it could survive outside the womb, when there is higher brain development. Fascinating speculation, but similar to arguments over the number of angels that could dance on a pinhead. The precise moment when the fetus becomes a person is less important than a simple acknowledgment that whatever category of human life the fetus is, it nonetheless has value; it is not nothing.

In most people's eyes, "personhood" is a code word for "extent of value," not a fine scientific fact. What those who favor abortion rights are saying is that whatever value fetal life has—from none to much—it is not the moral equivalent of those of us who have been born. In fact, pro-choicers argue, there are a number of values greater than the fetus that justify answering the "Who decides?" question strongly in favor of the woman.

However, once one moves away from the narrow question of when the fetus becomes a person to the more meaningful question of what value the fetus has and when that value emerges, it becomes difficult to develop an ethical formula for assigning value and asserting the obligations that flow from that value. There is a wide range of respectable opinion on these questions and few hard-and-fast conclusions.

AN URGENT TASK

But the need to offer some answers from a pro-choice perspective is both morally and politically urgent. Those opposed to abortion have moved aggressively for laws that depend on the recognition of the fetus as a person—as a rights-bearing entity. At the same time, there are scientific advances that affect the way we think about the fetus and indeed make it more present among us. For some, these realities lead to a greater connection to fetal life, perhaps not as a person, but as part of the continuum of what we are, of humanity. Examples include 3-D and 4-D pictures of fetuses in utero that appear to be awake, asleep, sucking, yawning—engaging in activities that are related to human identity—and the few very premature babies who struggle and appear to have a great determination to live. Even the reality that pre-embryos used to create stem cells that may ultimately save the lives of thousands makes the embryo more human and more valuable—it can give as well as receive, even at a stage of development that bears little resemblance even to fetal life. Of course, there is an element of my ode to the embryo that is poetic and romantic, even anthropomorphic, as the embryo does not consciously "give"; it is instead useful, but nonetheless that usefulness is a positive quality that should not be feared, but appreciated.

The fetus is indeed a wondrous part of our humanity; we are drawn to it as part of the ongoing mystery of who we are. Do we not question our own value and why we are here, what we contribute and what we take from the world? There is, of course, a danger in overromanticizing fetal life or in defining its value primarily in relation to ourselves. For an infertile couple who deeply want a child, someone else's fetus is very precious, and potentially their child. For a woman who has been raped, that fetus may well be seen as a monster. The relation of value to wantedness is complex and at times troubling. Anti-abortion groups have countered the "Every child a wanted child" message by pointing out that if wantedness is what gives us value and a right to life, then who among the unwanted will be the next to be declared disposable—the sick, the disabled, the poor, or the unemployed?

TOO HARD?

Such concerns should not be quickly dismissed. I am deeply struck by the number of thoughtful, progressive people who have been turned off to the pro-choice movement because of the lack of adequate and clear expressions of respect for fetal life; people who are themselves grappling with the conflict between upholding women's rights and the right to conscience and respecting the value of nascent human life. John Garvey, writing in *Commonweal*, put it well: "Our attitude toward life at this stage has much to say about what we believe about humanity as a whole: this is where we all come from, and at no point does it mean nothing." Garvey suggests that perhaps there has been a "hardening of the heart" resulting from the pro-choice position.

The John Garveys of the world have a point. They are not the enemies of choice. They occupy the middle ground that we seek to convince that being pro-choice is morally sound, and they sometimes express the wisdom of those who can see different sides in a moral dilemma.

Garvey's comments are suggestive of the last of the three values I believe must be included in an ethical pro-choice perspective: avoiding a coarsening of humanity that can result from the taking of life. Pro-choice advocates may bristle at such a claim; we see ourselves as deeply compassionate and good people who are working hard to alleviate women's pain and to create a world in which children are wanted and loved. How could anyone suggest that our sensibilities could become coarsened by exposure to the taking of fetal life that is currently a necessary component of abortion?

And, while little research has been done on this question, it and history points to no coarsening of respect for persons as a result of legal abortion. Those countries with long-standing liberal abortion laws have been among the most supportive of life. Japan, for example, widely uses abortion as a method of birth control. Yet the respect the Japanese show for the elderly is great and their love of children renowned. While abortion is common in Japan, there are rituals of respect for both aborted and miscarried fetuses that express value. The Scandinavian countries have liberal abortion laws and some of the most people-friendly social policies in the world. There is more evidence that denying women the right to choose abortion leads to a coarsening of attitudes toward children than permitting it does. In Ceauşescu's Romania, abortion was strictly forbidden and women's pregnancies monitored closely to prevent abortion. The resulting massive abandonment of children is well-known. Likewise, studies of children born after their mothers were denied abortion in the former Czechoslovakia and several Scandinavian countries show that these children have a significantly higher rate of crime, mental illness, and problems in school.

For me, a more troubling question is whether or not regular exposure to the taking of life in abortion or the defense of a right to choose abortion would, if not addressed, lead to a coarsening of attitude toward fetal life. The inability of pro-choice leaders to give any specific examples of ways in which respect for fetal life can be demonstrated, or to express any doubt about any aspect of abortion, suggests that such a hardening of the heart is possible. This concern or possibility does not lead me to say that abortion should become illegal, more restricted, more stigmatized. It does lead me to believe that we would do well as pro-choice people to present abortion as a complex issue that involves loss—and to be saddened by that loss at the same time we affirm and support women's decisions to end pregnancies. Is there not a way to simply say, "Yes, it is sad, unfortunate, tragic (or whatever word you are comfortable with) that this life could not come to fruition. It is sad that we live in a world where there is so little social and economic support for families that many women have no choice but to end pregnancies. It is sad that so many women do not have access to contraception. It is sad that this fetus was not healthy enough to survive, and it was good that this woman had the right to make this choice for herself and her family, to avoid suffering, and to act on her values and her sense of what her life should be?"

Are there not ways to affirm and protect the right to choose abortion while actively promoting policies which would actually enhance reflection and good decision-making and support voluntary mechanisms for nonjudgmental reflection and alternatives to abortion? For example, should we not combine our support for the right of adolescent girls to decide to have an abortion with greater efforts to involve their parents, including seeking funding for counseling for teens facing the abortion decision and their parents as an alternative to mandatory parental-consent and-notification laws? Surely we agree that young women aged thirteen, fourteen, fifteen (and even older) need their parents at this time? And surely, our response to date, which implies that only teens who are at risk from their parents choose not to tell them, rings hollow in the ears of most parents who know that their kids are loath to tell them where they are going on Saturday afternoon, let alone that they are pregnant. The youngest of teens should not have to face an abortion or any medical procedure alone. This is not just about rights; it is a matter of health, safety, and compassion.

RESPONDING TO ANTI-CHOICE LEGISLATION

There are many examples of ways in which those of us who are pro-choice could have better responded to unreasonable legislative initiatives by those who are anti-abortion, but two are at the top of my list: how we dealt with legislation regarding so-called partial-birth abortion and how we should deal with upcoming legislation on the provision of fetal anesthesia in abortions after twenty weeks' gestation.

It has long been a strategy of those opposed to legal abortion to concentrate on second- and third-trimester abortions, despite the fact that few abortions occur in the third trimester and a very small number in the second trimester. According to the latest figures available, 88 percent of abortions are performed in the first trimester (up to twelve weeks), just over 10 percent are performed between thirteen and twenty weeks, 2 percent after twenty weeks and only 0.08 percent in the third trimester (after twenty-four weeks). Among those who do not believe that fetuses are persons from the moment of conception (and the "moment of conception" is a dubious concept), there is a commonsense insight that fetal life gains in value as it develops capacity and physical structure and the ability to survive outside a woman's body. There is a sense that more significant moral justification is necessary for abortions later in pregnancy at the same time as one might hold that those justifications need not be subject to law.

If only, anti-abortion leaders say, people knew what happens in an abortion, they would turn against abortion with revulsion. Thus, some ten years ago, legislation was introduced to ban a procedure known medically as intact dilation and extraction except in cases where the woman's life was at risk. It is not easy to isolate this procedure from a continuum of abortion techniques used after about fifteen weeks of pregnancy, and the legislation fails to do so, creating a serious obstacle to its implementation. Nonetheless, all methods of abortion along this continuum are grim, as, frankly, are all late-term abortion procedures. There is nothing aesthetically attractive about the abortion of fully formed, relatively well-developed fetuses and there is equally nothing simple and painless about the situations women face that lead them to seek abortions later in gestation.

There is much blame to be placed at the door of anti-abortion leaders who sought this legislation. In fact, they showed little interest in crafting a bill that would be constitutionally accepted and thus save fetal life. Instead they opted to use the bill as an educational tool—a crass attempt to bombard society with gruesome visual images. The legislation was also dishonest. It tried to use a method of abortion as a surrogate for a desire to ban ultimately all abortions and immediately all post-first-trimester abortions. Moreover, had it contained an exception allowing the continuum of procedures to be performed if a woman's health was at risk, it might even have passed constitutional muster and effectively, if tragically, banned many medically indicated abortions, particularly those performed primarily due to serious damage to fetuses that made it likely or certain that they would not survive birth or have only a short, painful life.

Responding to such traps is not easy for those who are pro-choice, but our movement, as is often the case, did an excellent job in the courts pointing out the legal and constitutional flaws of the legislation. We failed miserably, however, to touch on the broader unrest about abortion itself that the procedure raised in the minds of many. The movement, some felt, goes too far when it defends such gruesome procedures. The pro-choice movement will be far more trusted if it openly acknowledges that the abortion decision involves weighing multiple values and that one of those values is fetal life. These acknowledgments must be made at the same time and with the same vigor that bad legislation is criticized and fought.

In the world in which I move, people who support legal abortion do not believe that discussing the morality of abortion is an act of treachery. They do not believe that to suggest that some abortions may happen for less-than-admirable reasons and to question some behaviors that lead to abortions is anti-woman or anti-abortion. In this world, people are waiting for some sign that pro-choice advocates are not pro-abortion, that we are sensitive to the values that are in conflict when abortion is considered or performed. And the lack of concern for fetal life and the gruesome nature of late-term abortion procedures in our response to the "partial-birth abortion" debate has pushed some potential supporters over the edge. Is there nothing, they ask, that concerns pro-choice people about abortion?

The intact dilation and extraction debate has about run its course. Pro-choice forces have won the legal argument again and again, as we should. The most recent attempt at legislation will most likely be ruled unconstitutional. But the question remains whether we emerge from the debate having won any hearts and minds. Who looks extreme in the strategic tug-of-war between pro-choice and anti-abortion forces—in which characterizing the other side as extremists is a key, if less-than-admirable goal?

HONORING LAW AND MORALITY

It has long been a truism of the abortion debate that those who are pro-choice have rights and those who are against legal abortion have morality; that those who support abortion rights concentrate on women and those opposed focus on the fetus. After thirty years of legal abortion and a debate that shows no signs of ending and has no clear winner, is it not time to try and combine rights and morality, to consider both women *and* developing human life? Ultimately, abortion is not a political question, and politics will not end the enormous conflict over abortion. Abortion is a profoundly moral question, and any movement that fails to grapple with and respect all the values at stake in crafting a social policy about abortion will be inadequate in its effort to win the support of the majority of Americans.

"I HAD AN ABORTION" AND OTHER ULULATIONS

JACQUELINE LALLEY

WHY SHOULD YOU LISTEN TO WHAT I HAVE TO SAY ABOUT REPRODUC-
tive rights? I'm not a policymaker, an academic, or even an activist, in
the chaining-yourself-to-a-fence sense of the word. I'm just a woman who
doesn't want to have fifteen kids. That's how many children a woman
could have if she didn't have access to birth control and abortion.[1] And
right-wing conservatives are doing their best to take away both.

Hey, did you see what I just did? I just made myself seem normal and
showed that people who oppose reproductive rights are not. I did it by
framing the issue using language. I wish I could take credit for this "framing" concept, I really do. I've always wanted to go on the lecture circuit
and hang with the lecture-circuit crowd. But the whole idea of framing
comes courtesy of Professor George Lakoff, and the Rockridge Institute.
He defines a frame as a mental structure that shapes the way we view the

world. Anyone who has successfully promoted a reproductive rights initiative has done so by understanding conservative or progressive values and creating a frame for reproductive rights that activates those values.

Understand framing and you'll understand how right-wing conservatives have gained so much control in the past few decades. They've waged a cultural war in our nation, and abortion is just one of many fronts in that war. For many women, and many progressives in general, it's an important front.

We can end this war. We just have to change the way we talk. And that means changing the way we think.

TALKING ABOUT VALUES

One metaphor that's been used to describe how the Right is working to take away our reproductive rights is the term "chipping away." Gloria Feldt, the former president of Planned Parenthood Federation of America, provides an impressive, comprehensive account of all of the federal- and state-level policies that comprise these "chips" in her book *The War on Choice*.

If the right wing is chipping, they're using a massive chisel to do it, and that chisel is morals and values. George Lakoff studied conservative and progressive values using linguistic methodology. He's written volumes about these values, but I'm going to sum them up in a couple of sentences:

Conservatives believe that the world is dangerous and there is evil out there, so what America needs is a strict father who can: (1) protect the family, (2) support the family, and (3) teach his children right from wrong by punishing them when they do wrong. These are "strict parent" values, and they are applied to actual families as well as to our nation.

But guess what? Progressives have values, too. Those values hold that the world can be made a better place, and it is our job to work to do that. The world needs a nurturing parent who can take care of children by: (1) empathizing with them and (2) taking responsibility for our own well-being and theirs. These are "nurturant parent" values. They, too, are applied to families and our nation.

Conservatives hold strict-father values in all spheres—at work, at home, in public, and in private. Progressives hold nurturant-parent values in all spheres. But these two groups make up only two-thirds of the American public. For the other third, these sets of values are active in different spheres.

So when we frame reproductive rights, we have to do it in such a way that we're activating the nurturant-parent values of progressives *and of that middle third.* That's what the conservatives have done, only with strict-father values.

When it comes to defending and expanding reproductive rights, the numbers are on our side. At least 90 percent of women in the United States have used birth control. At least one-third of women will have had an abortion by age forty-five.[2] Fertility is not a progressive phenomenon. People of all worldviews make use of their reproductive rights. But that doesn't mean they've been willing to fight to preserve them.

How Conservatives Talk About Abortion

Let's get this straight: Conservatives who are crafting political strategy don't really care about abortion. They're using it to forge a schism between progressives and the middle third and to convince the latter to adopt a more conservative worldview—one that makes a very small number of people very rich by cutting social programs and taxes, privatizing everything, and legalizing the rape of the earth.

How are they doing this? Not by controlling the Supreme Court. Not by passing legislation. Not by bombing abortion clinics and killing women's healthcare providers. True, the Right is using all of these tactics. And yes, these tactics are an important part of their campaign to take away both birth control and abortion, leaving women to "choose" between having fifteen children and not having sex. (If you want the details, and I hope you do, read *The War On Choice*.) But what has made these tactics possible is language. Conservatives at think tanks in Washington, D.C., are hard at work framing reproductive rights and other issues in ways that appeal to people with conservative values. Once their language is used and disseminated via the media, the names of bills they propose, and other avenues, their values are embedded in any discussion of the issue.

"Partial-birth abortion" is a good example. What does the "partial" refer to? It claims that the procedure is part birth, and for there to be a birth, there has to be not only a fetus but a baby. Putting "abortion" next to "partial-birth" is tantamount to calling anyone involved in this procedure a baby killer. In proposing a ban on late-term abortion, the right wing has used their name for the procedure—partial-birth abortion—combined with diagrams showing how the procedure is performed, and they have harped on the fact that the brain of the fetus is removed. This frame activates the strict-father value of needing to punish women who have had sex by painting them as brutal killers.

What's significant, however, is what the right wing has left out of the frame: that this procedure constitutes less than one percent of all abortions.[3] And, even more significantly, it is primarily performed when the woman's health is at great risk and/or if the fetus would not survive after birth. A great number of women who need this procedure are married and already have children. An accurate frame for these abortions would imply these facts. It would make clear that the extremity of the procedure is matched by the extremity of the medical risk if childbirth occurred. Using this frame, we might call the procedure "emergency abortion." This term builds on values of responsibility and empathy. In an emergency, we are bound to help. We empathize with a person facing a medical emergency. Abortion has to be available for these people.

Right-wingers know their frames will stick where their "facts" fail.

In the early 2000s, news media reported the story of Melanie Mills, who had an abortion procedure in Granite City, Illinois, in 1998. She later said she had obtained "pathology reports" (medical records) showing she had "never been pregnant" but instead had "suffered from a blighted ovum." She blamed her provider for carrying out the procedure when she was not pregnant, a claim that initiated lawsuits and a state investigation. Her provider waged a lawsuit to defend himself and his clinic. In 2005, an organization called Priests for Life circulated a news release claiming that the woman's experience typified two "common abuses" perpetrated by abortion providers: performing abortions on women who are not pregnant and intimidating women into silence about such malpractice.

How right-wing anti-rights activists used this frame is a case study in polemics. As with "partial-birth abortion," they used language to obscure the truth and provoke a strong public reaction.

The Priests for Life statement declared that Mills had a blighted ovum. In the medical profession, this condition is called an anembryonic pregnancy, and it occurs when a fertilized egg stops developing because the chromosomes are abnormal. By claiming that she wasn't pregnant, but only had a blighted ovum, Mills was saying, "I wasn't pregnant, but I was pregnant." Women often choose to have such an ovum removed via dilation and curettage (D&C), the same procedure used in most abortions. The March of Dimes (whose slogan is "Saving babies, together") recommends that in the case of an anembryonic pregnancy, "a woman and her provider choose the approach that is best for her"—waiting until the tissue is expelled via miscarriage, or having a D&C.

The first claim of Priests for Life—that abortion providers engage in malpractice by performing procedures on women who aren't pregnant—was contradicted by the facts of the case. Their second claim, that providers silence women about malpractice, was made moot by the lack of validity of the first claim.

Everything in this story hinged on the reader's ignorance of what a blighted ovum is. Did anyone who read their statement or the media coverage bother to look up the term? Not likely. Reporters writing about the story avoided the very common medical term "anembryonic pregnancy," perhaps taking their cue from press releases issued by the Right. The facts were wrong, but readers were able to disregard them because they were presented in a familiar frame: Women are vulnerable and need to be protected from those who would exploit or intimidate them.

But who was guilty of intimidation? The anti-rights movement used this story to intimidate a doctor who worked as an OB/GYN at a Catholic hospital and ran a safe, legal, comprehensive women's health clinic across the street. They didn't like the values this symbolized: tolerance, diversity, and separation of church and state. Religious institution on one side of the street, secular on the other. And so they attacked, invoking the image of the vulnerable woman. This same provider had been pictured on the famous WANTED posters issued by the American Coalition of Life Activists in 1995, used to encourage the murder of providers of legal abortions.

After the damage had already been done to the doctor's reputation, the state found that Mills's case was completely groundless and dismissed it.

Right-wing conservatives use polemics and lies to get their way, and that is clearly wrong. In no way am I suggesting that progressives follow suit. But progressives have much to learn from how the Right has used values: It has articulated them, built internal consensus around them, and mobilized large numbers of Americans by proudly broadcasting them. Progressives must do the same if reproductive rights are to survive.

HOW PROGRESSIVES TALK ABOUT ABORTION

Again, for right-wing conservative leaders, abortion is a wedge issue that's being used to draw people into their worldview. They don't really care about abortion, or birth control, for that matter.

Do progressives care? Um, yeah. The right to control our reproduction is vital to Americans' ability to do all of the things that spring from progressive values. Women and men are equals, and women should have careers and equal participation in public life. Deciding whether and when to have children is central to that goal. Moreover, progressives believe that it's our right and, in fact, our responsibility, to be happy. According to Lakoff, if you are unhappy, you won't want other people to be happy, and you won't work to make that happen. And unless you happen to be, say, Karl Rove's wife, sex makes you happy.

Progressives discourse on reproductive rights starts with how we refer to ourselves and our opponents. We refuse to call people who oppose reproductive rights "pro-life" because the majority of those people are also cutting public investments in health, education, and other supports needed by children. Usually, we call ourselves "pro-choice" and right-wingers "anti-choice." I am not crazy about the term "choice." It sounds like a luxury to me. What I want is the right to control my reproduction, and that right is under attack. I favor "pro-reproductive rights," which can be shortened to "pro-rights."

In the face of what amounts to a right-wing attack on sex, progressives do what is called "issue-based organizing." We go door-to-door and make phone calls, and we contact our representatives. Most of this is in response to bills that right-wingers are proposing that have names like "Partial-Birth Abortion Ban Act." It's hard to put your own frame on an issue when you're speaking in response to someone else's, but Planned Parenthood does a good job. In Wisconsin, the Right wrote and proposed SB 155, which would allow pharmacists to deny women birth-control pills. Pro-Life Wisconsin called it the "Pharmacists Conscience Clause Bill." Planned Parenthood of Wisconsin called it the "Prescription Denial Bill."

Because most of our messages are in response to right-wing legislative attempts, we talk about abortion separately from birth control.

But the Right is attempting to take away both, and they're lying about doing it. We need to talk about comprehensive reproductive rights. We need to talk about basic women's healthcare—which includes exams and tests, birth control, and abortion. We need to expose the Right's efforts to remove access to all of these things. By doing so, we can create a powerful coalition between abortion-rights activists and the more than 90 percent of women[4] (and very large percentage of men) who have depended on birth control over the course of their sexual lives.

Aside from content, there is the issue of tone. Progressives tend to bog down our messages with details about policies and programs. We need to back up and frame the issues themselves, using our values. And we need to make our statements bold. One laudable effort in this regard was the I HAD AN ABORTION T-shirt produced by Planned Parenthood. This slogan was aimed at depriving the antirights movement of the "personal dispensation" mentality that has gained them support from the middle third. Many women and men feel that abortion—and even birth control—are okay for them, but not for other people. They'll use birth control, but say high school students shouldn't even learn about it. They'll have an abortion—or support their wives, girlfriends, sisters, etc., in doing so—but oppose the legality and morality of abortion. Staff members at women's health clinics regularly see women who have just had abortions join the antirights protestors on the sidewalk.

"I had an abortion" really means, "If you had an abortion, I defend and support you, and I expect the same from you." That's a nurturant mentality, one of mutual respect. It's a progressive way of framing the issue. It's also a "coming-out" frame: People close to the individual "coming out" become invested in reproductive rights because of that particular individual. Of course, someone who holds strict-father values may reject the woman. But thousands of women were willing to take that risk; Planned Parenthood sold out of the T-shirts.

The I HAD AN ABORTION T-shirt raises some good questions. Why aren't progressive men wearing T-shirts that say MY GIRLFRIEND/WIFE HAD AN ABORTION? Why are women alone expected to make this personal information public, for the cause of reproductive rights? But the fact is that only by doing so can we remove shame, and when we do away with shame we can remove the need for personal dispensations—which are the only thing that makes it possible for the middle third to protest or ignore reproductive rights.

One last message that I want to touch on briefly can be paraphrased as, "Legal abortion protects women from back-alley butchers." There are two problems with this message, which is widely disseminated by progressives: First, it is not true that large numbers of abortion providers in the United States were endangering or killing women when they carried out illegal procedures prior to *Roe v. Wade*. Most of these providers were well-trained and safe and were bravely putting themselves at risk to perform the abortions that women needed. And abortion providers will do so again if and when *Roe v. Wade* is overturned or eviscerated. To say otherwise is to alienate an important group of pro-rights activists, and to terrorize women who need abortions under circumstances in which they are illegal. The second and more important danger is that this message hides the fact that, by far, the largest risk to women before *Roe v. Wade* was self-performed abortions. It is much safer for a woman to have an illegal abortion from a trained ally than to maim, poison, sterilize, and/or kill herself in an attempt to end her pregnancy by herself.[5]

When I talk to professionals who have made it their job to promote reproductive rights, such as the staff of Planned Parenthood affiliates and NARAL Pro-Choice America, I am heartened. They are bold, they are aggressive, and they are doing their best with limited funding to broadcast progressive values and be on the offensive, not the defensive. But it's scary how underresourced they are compared to organizations working for the Right. Progressives need to give more money to think tanks and the policy arms of organizations like Planned Parenthood. These organizations can generate and coordinate the dissemination of progressive, pro-rights value statements among progressives and the middle third.

CREATING FRAMES THAT EXPAND REPRODUCTIVE RIGHTS

As progressives, it is imperative that we talk about what we believe in, what kind of world we want to live in, and what kind of world we want future generations to live in. Leading up to the 2004 presidential election, with the foul breath of George W. Bush on our necks, we cowered behind Kerry's culturally conservative speeches and mannerisms. We talked about facts and programs instead of boldly proclaiming our progressive values.

What are these values? Luckily, Prof. Lakoff has already done the work to define them, saving me at least five years and the hundreds of thousands of dollars it would cost me to get a PhD. Based on his extensive research and work with political leaders, we know that progressive values are:

1. Empathy
2. Responsibility

These, in turn, imply the following, for a total of ten progressive values:

3. Freedom
4. Opportunity
5. Prosperity
6. Fairness
7. Honesty
8. Communication that is open and goes two ways
9. Community: building it, serving it, and cooperating within it
10. Trust

When I read these, they seemed self-evident—the universal norm. But they're not, and thinking that they are has gotten progressives into a lot of trouble. That belief has led us to assume that our worldview is "common sense," when in fact conservative values are based on a totally different worldview. Their strict-parent model starts with the idea that every misfortune that befalls an individual is brought on by his or her moral weakness. The sooner we realize that, the sooner we can put our own values clearly on the table and use them to attract new allies and accomplish our goals.

Frames that invoke these values can unify progressives and the middle third, who together comprise a clear majority of the U.S. population. We must not shift to the right in the hopes of enlisting the support of right-wingers. They want to force us to have fifteen children apiece, remember? They demonize and even kill doctors who provide safe, legal abortions. Trying to reason with them is like negotiating with terrorists or telemarketers.

Here are some values-based frames that we could use to secure and protect reproductive rights—and activate the worldview of progressives and the middle third. These are lines of reasoning and statements of common sense. They are not in and of themselves text for public awareness campaigns or advertisements, but they can be the basis for such vehicles for change:

Freedom: Decisions about whether and when to have children are life-changing. As individuals and families, we are free to make those decisions ourselves. Why would we ever want to hand over that freedom to politicians?

Every American is free to pursue an education and a fulfilling career. Telling women how many children they have to have, and when, and under what circumstances, takes that freedom away from women, creating a second class of citizens.

Responsibility: We are responsible for our own actions. Women

WHAT, ME, OPPOSE BIRTH CONTROL?

If the vast majority of Americans use or have used birth control, and most support the right to have an abortion, how are right-wingers like Right to Life getting support for their radical legislation, which would make both birth control and abortion crimes? They're giving massive amounts of money to the Republican Party for its candidates' campaigns, and in exchange, these officials are introducing, proposing, and voting for bills that these groups draft themselves.

In 2005, Representative Robin Vos (R-Wisc.) supported AB 285, the Prescription Denial Bill. The bill was drafted by Wisconsin Right to Life and would make it legal for pharmacists to deny women the Pill. When Planned Parenthood of Wisconsin publicized his support of the bill with an ad in a local newspaper, Vos said it was mistaken. "I'm a single guy," he said. "To say I am against birth control is to say I am against water." Of course, Planned Parenthood proved publicly that his name was on that bill, as well as numerous others drafted by Wisconsin Right to Life. Then, suddenly, AB 285 was back in committee, and plans to vote on it were tabled.

From Vos's point of view, the episode was a disaster: He lost progressive voters' support, and the Republican Party is no doubt displeased with his pro-rights statements. But what happened to Vos can only be useful to the extent that progressives publicize it as just one of myriad examples of our elected representatives acting against the wishes of their constituents for the sake of their careers. They're pimping our reproductive rights for a shot at power.

and their partners use birth control or decide to have an abortion because it's the responsible thing to do. Women are expected to pay taxes and vote, and many are defending our nation in the military. We need to have laws that enable women to make responsible decisions about when and under what circumstances to have children.

Empathy: It is barbaric to force a woman who has been raped to have a child as a consequence of that rape. These women have been traumatized, and their independence has been taken away from them by criminals. They need our empathy, our support, and our help in regaining their well-being and independence.

Likewise, it is cruel to make a woman give birth when she is too ill to have and raise a child, or when she is so ill that childbirth may kill her, or when the baby would be born dead. We cannot turn our backs on these women and their families.

Honesty and Two-Way Communication: Our elected officials are betraying us. They're taking campaign contributions from right-wing groups and, in exchange, promoting laws that deny us access to birth control and abortion. Our elected officials work for us. They need to represent our interests. They can't get away with betraying us.

MY STORY

January 20, 2005, was two days before the anniversary of *Roe v. Wade.*

George W. Bush was being inaugurated as President of the United States of America for the second time.

Anti-consumerist groups were holding a Buy Nothing Day to protest the inauguration.

And I was having an abortion.

While I was waiting on the operating table, the nurse made small talk. "So, did you spend any money today?" she asked, referring to Buy Nothing Day.

"Yeah, $375," I said, referring to my final payment down at the front desk.

She winced. Then she gave me the first of about a million nuanced smiles. I changed the subject by bringing up *Roe v. Wade,* and she told me about all the times—over more than thirty years—that she'd helped women make it through crowds of violent protestors and get the health-care they needed. Her stories made me think the world of her. More people should hear those stories. They make clear just how hard we have worked together to protect the rights that are ours by law.

I hadn't chosen to have the abortion on this significant date deliberately. Like most people, I scheduled it as soon as possible once I'd made my decision. And like most people, I was miserable and distraught about having to end a pregnancy.

But I was also incredibly relieved. Relieved that I was going to get my life back, and that the law still made that possible. Even though conservatives were, at that very hour, ramping up for another four years of trying to take away that right, women still had it, and reasonable people nationwide would continue to fight for it. Our words—the way we frame the issues and tell our stories—are our best chance at winning.

TWICE IS A SPANKING

JENNIFER BAUMGARDNER

MY FRIEND MARION BANZHAF IS THE KIND OF FEMINIST WHO WEARS an I HAD AN ABORTION T-shirt with TALK TO ME scrawled by hand beneath the message. She worked at feminist health centers throughout the 1970s where she demonstrated vaginal self-exams and performed menstrual extractions. She was a pioneering member of the AIDS activist group ACT UP in its 1980s heyday. She recounts the story of her abortion in a 2005 film I produced called *Speak Out: I Had an Abortion*. The year was 1971, and there were only a couple of states, notably New York, where abortion was legal. Although her boyfriend thought they should drop out of school at the University of Florida and get married—they could live with his mother—Marion disagreed. She raised the money for her abortion in one afternoon by standing on the quad, asking for donations. She then flew from Gainesville to New York, had her abortion, and after she left the clinic, ran skipping down the street. "I was *so* happy to see that blood," she says in a trademark Marion Banzhaf way (somewhat shocking, totally confident). "It meant I had my life back."

Dauntless radical though she is, there is a part of her abortion story she rarely tells. A year after her 1971 procedure, Marion got pregnant again. This time she didn't have to worry about the money. Her new boyfriend pulled out his checkbook and put her on the next flight— again she knew it was the right decision. "But it was a much harder [abortion] for me personally. I felt I shouldn't have let myself get pregnant," says Marion, now fifty-two. "Even to this day, I have shame about it. An accomplished consciousness-raised feminist like me!"

One abortion—that happens. Two? Well, to paraphrase Oscar Wilde, two smacks of carelessness. My father, a doctor in Fargo, North Dakota, expressed surprise when I mentioned the second-abortion stigma to him: "It's odd, given that it's the exact same situation as before, no more or less of a life," my father said. "It's as if women don't *really* believe they have the right to have abortions." Dad, like Marion, is often shockingly logical. Still, abortion itself (whether your first or fourth) is so shrouded in secrecy, it's easy to imagine that only certain kinds of women would ever make a mistake like that *twice*. If she did need another abortion, the almost-unconscious thinking goes, it's clear she didn't care enough to learn from the first one. Fears about these repeat cases contribute to the unlovely idea that, because terminating a pregnancy is legal, women use abortion as birth control, leading to a cliché of this debate: the "I'm pro-choice, but I don't think it should be used as birth control" line.

In the clinic world, repeat visitors are called, not unkindly, "frequent flyers." The reason that casual term is not an insult is simply due to how common multiple abortions are. The Guttmacher Institute, one of the most-respected research facilities focusing on reproductive health, estimates that "if a sexually active woman were to use abortion as her means of birth control and wanted two children, she would have about thirty abortions by the time she reached age forty-five." By contrast, although almost half of the women who will have an abortion this year will have had one previously,[1] a more typical number of repeats is two or three—hardly constituting a disavowal of responsible contraception.

"You have 300 possibilities to get pregnant in your life," says Peg Johnston, the director of an abortion clinic in Binghamton, New York. "A 1 percent failure rate—assuming the best possible use of contraception—is still three abortions," she says. "In what endeavor," asks Johnston, "is a 1 percent failure rate not acceptable?" Sensible, it's true—and yet virtually everyone I have talked to about the issue of multiple abortions said that the woman shouldn't have let it happen again, implying it was her fault.

Why is that? Well, some of it is surely our anti-woman culture, along with a robust pro-life movement that, when abortion became legal, mobilized to scream at women on what is already not a fun day. But it's not just a vast right-wing conspiracy. Many women—pro-choice women—believe that abortion is taking a life (although not an independent life). What justifies that loss of life is the woman's *own* life. It's almost as if she is saying, "I recognize that this is serious, but my own life is too important to sacrifice for an unplanned pregnancy." But with each additional abortion, it is harder for some women to believe they are making an honorable decision.

Or that *he* is. My friend Matt, like many men in my life, has been part of more than one abortion. When he was younger, he was "knee-jerk pro-choice." If an unplanned pregnancy occurs in high school or college, he figured, of course you have an abortion. That's just common sense. He didn't revisit those thoughts with any sort of introspection until his first abortion experience, "but I wasn't in love with [the woman in question], we had no future together, I was comfortable saying we need to abort," Matt concludes. "I gave her money. She didn't express any need for me to be there with her." He says, bluntly, that his second abortion experience, last year, felt "more like murder," and that he was disgusted at himself for being the reason his girl was at Planned Parenthood confronting scary toothless protesters and enduring this awful day. The circumstances had changed—Matt did have a future with the woman he got pregnant with, although having a baby just then, a few months into their relationship, wasn't a good idea at all. Mostly, though, it felt unseemly and immature to be there. "I sat at the clinic with all of these younger guys and I thought, 'I am too old to be here, man,' " says Matt, now thirty-eight. "When do I stop giving myself the out? That is what abortion feels like—a free pass. But it's not totally free. There are emotional consequences, and as you get older, the sense of taking responsibility for your actions grows."

"There is something in that moment where you are supposed to smarten up," agrees Jenny Egan, a twenty-five-year-old ACLU staffer who had an abortion at age sixteen. "That is your one fuck-up. Birth control can't fail and a condom can't break now." But, as Jenny points out, the shame is often not the choice of having the second abortion itself—it's not the idea of killing a second baby when we can only justify killing one—the shame is the shame of getting pregnant again. It means that you don't have enough control and power over your life to take care of yourself, especially when you've been there before.

Which brings us to a paradox of feminism. The success of the women's movement is not just in its overhaul of all of the institutions that kept women down—although it has made inroads in all of them, including national abortion rights, birth control for single people, and sexuality education (all under fire and the latter almost eradicated in favor of abstinence-only education). The more profound revolution was the raised expectations this once-utopian movement suggested to its daughters. The mantra of empowerment means that women feel like responsible actors in sex—not merely ignorant victims—and that knowledge makes it harder, in a way, to justify the mistake of unplanned pregnancy. *If you're so smart, if you read* Our Bodies, Ourselves *at age thirteen, if you knew about condoms, how come you got pregnant?*

Speak Out ends with dozens of women saying, "My name is ___, and I had an abortion." A few of them—an older matron, a curly-haired professor type—say, "I had two abortions." One woman says, "I had three abortions." At a recent screening, her presence provoked one young female audience member to wonder aloud why the multiple-abortion woman didn't use birth control and whether we, the filmmakers, should be promoting the idea that multiple abortions were as justified as one. At that same screening, a well-known second-wave feminist writer Alix Kates Shulman, replied to the requisite "where's the birth control?" comment by saying that she had had four abortions "and not one was the result of carelessness." A few audience members vigorously nodded their heads in a "hear, hear!" manner, but I had the sense that most people were quietly wondering if the woman who posed the question—pointing out that once is funny, but twice is a spanking—was right.

In September, at another screening of *Speak Out,* Pauline Bart, another second-wave woman of some reputation within the movement, suggested that younger women learn to do abortions themselves just as the women's collective known as "Jane" did pre-*Roe v. Wade.* "It's just like taking a melon baller and scooping out a melon," she said, referring to performing an abortion in one's own apartment. I nodded earnestly but thought, *No, it isn't.* Or, at least, it isn't to me. I don't doubt that some women experience abortion as equally devoid of angst as Pauline Bart depicted it, and that for them each abortion is created equal. For many women, though, getting pregnant when they don't want to signifies that they made a mistake. Often the mistake is not their own fault—Alix was not told by her doctor that diaphragms could slip out of place; Marion got depressed from the effects of the high-dose Pill and found it almost impossible to take. But if an abortion is meant to correct that mistake, is it anti-woman to presume a learning curve? I don't know. Fertility and sexuality are very complex. Let's be real—some people are better at birth control than others. After all, I've had unprotected sex more often than protected sex, so I'm hardly one to *tsk-tsk*.

Virtually everyone I have spoken to who has worked in a clinic has a story of one patient who had not two or three abortions, but twenty or more despite contraceptive counseling with each clinic visit. Johnston, who has thirty years experience in the clinics, thinks multiple abortions on that scale point to something larger than an individual snafu. Occasionally that larger thing is carelessness, but usually it's in the context of a life out of control in other ways—a woman who has several children already or women whose lives are chaotic and stressful in ways that are hard for many women to imagine. A history of sexual abuse can also play out in a woman's inability to take care of herself in matters of birth control.

Sadly, though, the most common reason for multiple abortions is that, at around $30 to $50 a month for the Pill, many women can't afford birth control. "I hear that all the time," says Johnston, noting that a majority of the forty-five million uninsured people in this country are women. Another longtime clinic director, Claire Keyes of Allegheny Reproductive Health Center, in Pittsburgh, Pennsylvania, told me that among women with insurance that covers birth control, the majority have policies that mandate generic pills, which are only required to contain 80 percent of the ingredients in brand-name birth control. When you consider the escalating average weights of women today, it is evident how this weaker dose is even more diluted—and both issues are unanalyzed contributions to birth-control failures. Meanwhile, according to Johnston, "Some people are really fertile and others simply have lots and lots of sex. Frankly, if you have a lot of sex, you'll get pregnant more often."

As for my friend Marion Banzhaf, she did find a way to make sure she didn't have another birth-control failure while still having lots of sex. Soon after her second abortion, she came out as a lesbian.

MORALITY PLAY

REBECCA TRAISTER

WHEN HILLARY RODHAM CLINTON ADDRESSED FAMILY PLANNING
Advocates of New York State on January 24, 2005, she surprised her
audience by talking about abortion as "a sad, even tragic choice to
many, many women." She called for advocates on both sides of the
bitter reproductive-rights divide to find "common ground." She reminded the crowd of her mid-1990s endorsement of "teen celibacy,"
and she reached out to those who have opposed reproductive freedoms
for women by saying, "I for one respect those who believe with all their
heart and conscience that there are no circumstances under which abortion should be available."

Clinton's remarks, on the heels of similar comments from leading
Democrats Howard Dean and John Kerry, were widely interpreted as
part of a post-election Democratic move toward the center, a wooing of

the nation's perceived "values voters." Some critics saw Clinton's speech as a betrayal of the pro-choice party line that has long been a part of the Democratic platform.

But the story is not simply about the direction of the Democratic Party. Clinton's sound bites may well have been a loud—possibly misinterpreted, certainly oversimplified—public signifier that a far more profound and uncomfortable discussion is heating up the women's movement itself. After years of intermittent jostling from the inside, a December 2004 essay, "Is There Life After *Roe?*" (a later version of which is included in this anthology on page 189) by Catholics for a Free Choice President Frances Kissling, on the value of the fetus seems to have cracked the hard ideological shell of the pro-choice community, exposing its messy theological, moral, and emotional innards. The resulting scramble may not be the end of a movement, but rather a chance at rebirth before what could be the fight of its life.

There have been a number of surprising—and divergent —eruptions in the pro-choice movement over the past couple of years from a group that has remained relatively on-message since the 1973 *Roe vs. Wade* victory. Since the passage of *Roe*, pro-choice advocates have been forced to maintain a defensive position, watching their victory seep away as anti-abortion activists push through piece after piece of restrictive legislation. The pro-life movement—energized by being on the losing end of *Roe*—has deftly tugged at American heartstrings by parading photos of bloody fetuses before the Senate and in front of clinics and by claiming the vocabulary of life and loss as its own.

Now many in the pro-choice community are looking to reclaim that language, to warm up what has come to be regarded as an absolutist, clinical, chilly movement with language that is emotional, conciliatory, moralistic, and even religious. In short, what the wildly different pro-choice projects launched in recent months have in common is a risky mission to put the heart back into the fight for abortion rights.

In January 2004, Alexander Sanger, chair of the International Planned Parenthood Council and grandson of the organization's founder, Margaret Sanger, published the book *Beyond Choice: Reproductive Freedom in the 21st Century*, in which he presented what he called "a very simple but heretical question. How many more pieces of anti-choice legislation will it take to get the pro-choice movement to rethink its approach to the issue?" He wrote, "I believe that to win the judicial battles and political battles we first must win the battle for the hearts and minds of the American people . . . If the American people have moral confusion about abortion, then the fault lies with [those of us] who argue on behalf of reproductive rights." The answer, Sanger went on to argue, is to reframe the debate in a way that makes clear that abortion is a moral choice, integral to the formation of happy, healthy families.

Some have been trying to preach a new gospel of abortion pride: Planned Parenthood sold T-shirts that proclaimed I HAD AN ABORTION; one activist started a website called I'mNotSorry.net.

In her 2004 essay, Kissling, a beloved figure in the women's movement whose thirty years as a pro-choice advocate and Catholic leader lends her both moral and ideological credibility, made the radical argument that the pro-choice movement must acknowledge the moral value of a fetus—and the potentially painful reality of its loss—in order to strengthen its claim that a woman's right to choose is ultimately worth more. Needless to say, the essay raised alarm on both sides of the abortion debate. Feminist Majority Foundation president Eleanor Smeal was quoted in the *Village Voice* as saying, "I don't buy it," suggesting that arguments like Kissling's distract advocates from the work of preventing women's suffering. And, she pointed out, "I don't hear [Kissling] saying that there's joy sometimes." Catholic League President William Donohue released a statement headlined "Pro-Abortion Camp Seeks to Hijack Religion."

Even the politicians are in on the act; Howard Dean has called on

Democrats to "change our vocabulary" about the abortion issue, while John Kerry acknowledged he believed that life begins at conception but still supports a woman's right to get an abortion.

Confronting the status of the fetus is a scary proposition for pro-choice advocates. To acknowledge it as anything other than a mass of developing cells is to risk careering down a slippery slope to the word "murder." To write or speak a sentence on the subject of abortion rights is to face a field of semantic land mines; every reference to a fetus or its potential future must be preceded by the appropriate conditional. Kissling understands this as well as anyone. I spoke to Kissling by phone, who recalled her work in clinics in the 1970s when women wanted to know, "Will my fetus feel pain?" Kissling paused and said, "and they didn't say 'fetus.' "

Even Kissling—willing to break many taboos—is unwilling to say that the word they used was "baby." Pro-choicers shy from "baby" in reference to unborn humans like horses from flames. That's precisely why the seemingly quiet notion of "changing vocabulary" within the debate has the potential to be explosive. That's also part of why work, like Kissling's, that asserts a language of feeling and loss regarding the termination of pregnancy has such an impact. "Is There Life After *Roe?*" struck a chord because it acknowledged an uncomfortable human truth: that for some happily, healthily expectant women—and even for some who abort their fetuses—the bump in their midsection is a baby.

"I think it makes all of us uncomfortable," said Kissling of her line of inquiry. "It is sometimes uncomfortable for me. How do we say this in ways that don't undercut our argument or aren't misinterpreted? This is a tough task, a difficult transition period." She added, "We have resisted the moral conversation for good reason. Historically, as well as in the present, the minute you raise morality, opponents of women's rights use it against us."

But, Kissling said, "I think it's pretty sad if the reality of pro-choice thought is that a discussion of morality leads to an anti-abortion position." Kissling has always trod the delicate line between her pro-choice compatriots and her Catholic belief. The Roman Catholic hierarchy remains the mortal enemy of reproductive freedom, be it abortion or birth control. "I've thought about the morality of this ad nauseam for thirty-five years, and come to the conclusion that making the choice [to have an abortion] can be a profoundly morally correct decision," said Kissling. "It can be morally incorrect too, but so can having a baby."

Kissling continued, "To me, a pro-choice movement that couldn't withstand moral scrutiny would be a very poor movement. And I don't think we have a poor movement." In fact, Kissling said that her essay stemmed in part from internal debate among pro-choice leaders—about how to reconcile changing medical and cultural views of the fetus with an abortion-rights agenda. In it, Kissling presents a philosophically challenging argument that requires intense consideration from its reader. It's not the kind of thing that translates smoothly to the political stage, especially in a glib, "Need some wood?" political era. If ethicists and theologians find it challenging to absorb a philosophy in which we accept a fetus's value as well as the value of a woman's choice to abort it, how can we reasonably expect an electorate intolerant of dependent clauses to take the time to hash it out? And what happens when politicians eager to jump on what looks like a new centrist bandwagon simplify the message until they transform it into something straight from the mouths of the religious Right?

Andrew Sullivan's article "Life Lesson," in the *New Republic,* written in response to Clinton's speech, congratulated the senator on asserting both that "the right to legal abortion should remain" and that "abortion is always and everywhere a moral tragedy." It included a few words on the "horrors of partial-birth abortion" and ended by proclaiming that in order to win a values debate, the Democrats need "a simple message: Saving one precious life at a time." Sullivan certainly is not the worst foe to face the pro-choice movement. Much about his piece is reasonable, especially his support for over-the-counter emergency contraception. And yet he slips into language that doesn't simply recognize a fetus but worships it.

This is part of what some consider dangerous about Kissling's work, or about Clinton's assertions about the "tragic choice" to abort. It's a reasonable desire to expand the discussion to recognize loss and conflict, but it should also be remembered that abortion is not always tragic or even complicated. Many women terminate pregnancies with joy and relief. Abortions, in addition to easing medical or economic problems, can mark the cessation of emotional and spiritual turmoil just as easily as they can provoke it. Many women feel no guilt at all.

Kissling—who said she was "willing to talk strategy" but insisted that her arguments were based on belief, not politics—said she thinks that nuance is the only way for the movement to once again grab America's attention. "It's only when you say something unexpected that you can even get people to listen to you. I have heard responses from Catholics who are neither pro-choice nor pro-life, who say, 'This is the first thing I've heard that makes me feel positively about the pro-choice movement.' I am not interested in the rank-and-file NARAL member. I am interested in the person who is conflicted about this issue."

By phone, *Beyond Choice* author Alexander Sanger spoke fondly of Kissling: "My only difference with Frances is that before we get to the theological we have to understand the biological. She skipped a step. That is understandable because she's coming from the Catholic perspective. But, discussions of the fetus are important to have and we have a right to understand what biology is doing in a pregnancy. Once we understand that, we can talk about how we draw a balance between the woman and her reproductive goals and the potential humanity of the fetus."

"But I think this discussion is long overdue," Sanger continued.

"We, me included, have been talking a certain way for the last thirty years. And public opinion polls have not changed one iota. The amount of legislation enacted that restricts women's access and demeans women continues to grow. We are not winning this battle."

Sanger said that on many levels, he has been pleased that politicians have begun to rethink the approach to abortion rights. "There is no question in my mind that we, the pro-choice movement, ought to be leading the way to reframing how we talk about abortion," he said. "So if various leaders of the Democratic Party are beginning to have this discussion, that is all to the good." But he warned, "We have to differentiate between the pro-choice movement and the Democratic Party." What the politicians are saying may be sound, but their strategy may be suspect. "The Democrats are looking for a scapegoat for the loss in [the November 2004 election], and they've picked the wrong one [in abortion]."

About Clinton, Sanger said: "Her speech was vintage Planned Parenthood for 98 percent of it. She was talking about prevention, and this is something we've been talking about for the last ninety years." On the other hand, he said: "I was disappointed that the value Hillary led off with is that abortion is bad. I don't believe we are ever going to win over the American public unless we make the case that abortion is a moral decision."

If the feeling among some leaders is that the movement is changing its footing, others were quick to smother the impact of Clinton's speech, as well as Kissling's essay. Feminist Majority Foundation president and former president of NOW Smeal didn't seem to think there was anything worth reporting. "You talk about a change in language," Smeal said by phone. "I read [Clinton's] whole speech and really she's been saying this for a long, long time. I don't think there's a change there." Smeal pooh-poohed what she called "that little sentence on 'common ground'—that's not new either. I was having 'common ground' meetings [with anti-abortion groups] in the '80s as a president of NOW."

Kate Michelman, who stepped down last year as president of NARAL Pro-Choice America, agreed. "It may sound new because Hillary chose to give it prime time, but it's not new," Michelman said. "Twenty-one years ago, when I was recruited for the presidency of NARAL, they asked me what kinds of things I thought were most important for the pro-choice movement to address. I said number one is our message, the way that we talk about what it means to be pro-choice. As a woman who had to make the choice [to abort], and who had three girls, the language of the movement didn't speak to me and at times sounded strident and not inclusive of the women who chose to have children. I felt we needed to communicate better what it meant to be pro-choice and the values that underlie a pro-choice position." Two years ago, NARAL (the National Abortion Rights Action League) changed its name to the less abortion-centric NARAL Pro-Choice America.

Michelman wrote a letter to *The New York Times* in the wake of Clinton's speech praising the senator for reaching out to anti-abortion advocates but cautioning, "As one who has reached across the ideological chasm on that basis for many years, I regret to say she may find that few on the other side are reaching back." Asked whether she thinks that politicians like Kerry and Clinton have jumped the gun by communicating a boiled-down version of the movement's internal debate, Michelman said, "In reality, it's going to happen simultaneously . . . and I think our movement must be partners in this with our political leaders."

That is, if you believe that anything new really is happening to begin with. Smeal again emphasized her no-news-here stance, speaking to a reality that has been used to both bolster and chip away at the choice movement: the unchanging polls. "The polls have been the same for thirty years," Smeal said. "And in reality, so is the debate. At various stages someone says something that seems different for two minutes and then you realize that it's just more of the same, like the Church's stand that abortion is immoral."

It's true that the movement has always implicitly included personal ambivalence about abortion under its "choice" umbrella. Starting with Margaret Sanger's assertion that every child should be a wanted child, family-planning advocates have always been family-friendly—in theory. But backed into a corner, forced to defend a hard legal line that cannot afford gray areas, they have sometimes found it easy to confuse "pro-choice" with "pro-abortion."

Smeal is right that Clinton, Dean, and Kissling are not exactly talking revolution. But she may also have an investment in behaving as if nothing new is being said. Clinton's dropping of the term "common ground" with reference to right-to-lifers in the wake of the election, in a media climate where all anyone can write about is the Left's attempts to make inroads into the red states, is surely calculated. This is gift-wrapped for the press for maximum exposure and impact. And that impact could alter perceptions about the strength and cohesion of the pro-choice movement—just as it must fight for pro-choice judges and address the possibility that *Roe* could be overturned and the abortion decision sent back to the states. It's a moment when perceived signs of discord are not good. As Smeal stressed with exasperation, "I feel like I'm chasing at windmills. Ever since the election, the press has been determined to start infighting on the liberal side."

She also pointed out a very real danger in the "make abortion rare" Clintonspeak: Nothing is going to change unless contraception becomes cheaper and more readily available to everyone, and that looks increasingly unlikely. While Smeal and her supporters advocate over-the-counter sales of birth-control pills and emergency contraception, several states have recently passed laws that allow pharmacists who don't believe in contraception to refuse to sell it to consumers.

As she considered the impact of a morality debate on the movement's ability to focus on more pressing medical concerns, Smeal became nearly apoplectic. "We're sitting around saying, 'Oh, is she a good girl or a bad girl?' It's sad for [some women], so they talk about morality when children in homes for unwanted children don't have clothing? I think that's sick. Children are naked and we're not doing anything about AIDS or clean water . . . So basically, I'm sick of reading about this. Am I a moral person? Come on! I was raised a Catholic! I was raised with this theology!"

Smeal's point here is compelling. Even if there were no legislative risks to pursuing questions of reproductive morality, doesn't it lay an additional burden on women who choose to abort? Why should we bring good-girl/bad-girl questions of guilt into it? Kissling's argument—not in response to Smeal, but in our earlier conversation—is, "Women are already having this conversation with themselves . . . Do you think women don't know there is something inside them? Duh. Come on. Do you think they are not bombarded with talk that is moralistic and negative every day? Do we not have something better to offer them in the way of moral framework? Women are dealing with this, and I don't think we should infantilize them."

Kissling also said, warning that she knew this response might sound "a little harsh": "I don't think that the right to choose abortion or the right to be treated as an autonomous, empowered woman means you are entitled never to hear anything that might be troubling . . . Life is not without its complexity. . . . In critical areas of moral inquiry we have to speak the full truth."

Asked whether the women's movement needs to make changes, Smeal said, "What the women's movement needs to do is put women back in the picture and put girls back in the picture. Because if [abortion becomes illegal again] girls and women will be maimed, they will die, they will be hurt, they will suffer needlessly."

Amy Richards, cofounder of the Third Wave Foundation, wrote in an email, "Sadly . . . the reaction to Clinton's remarks and Kissling's proposal seems to be resistance to understanding the current state of things, which is an evolution of abortion rights, not backpedaling." Later, by

phone, she said that Smeal and the other leaders of the pro-choice movement need to listen more to their constituents and what they're saying. "I
think she and they lived in a time when abortion was illegal, so they can
only foresee two scenarios: legal and illegal. But now there is confidence,
which they might describe as naiveté, on the part of younger women that
no one is going to take the right to an abortion from them."

Richards said that years ago, when approached by someone who
asked her if it was possible to be pro-life and a feminist, she said "absolutely not." "That's because I interpreted being pro-life as being anti-
women's choices," she said. "But what people were really saying is, 'Can
I be a feminist and be someone who is conflicted about this issue? Do I
have to say I'm pro-abortion?' And the answer to that is no."

"It's interesting that it's happening right now," Richards said of
what she perceives as the shifting attitudes within the movement, noting that Michelman's departure from NARAL earlier this year preceded Planned Parenthood President Gloria Feldt's resignation by two
weeks. Richards wondered if "this isn't a moment at which the old
guard is stepping down."

There are certainly generational land mines in a women's movement that hasn't been cohesive for generations. Younger women are
anxious to participate; they clogged the streets of Washington, D.C.,
during the April 2004 March for Women's Lives. But some may wonder what their role is. Technology and mating practices are not the only
things that have morphed over the decades; so has the attitude of the
generations of women who have grown up without fear of coat hang-
ers or back alleys. Smeal said that in her experiences on campuses—the
Feminist Majority Foundation is the major liaison between the movement and college kids—she has observed more anger. "Young women
are going to be tougher than any of us ever were. They have no hes-
itancy, no apology, no shame. They don't feel [abortion] is moral or
immoral. They feel it's necessary, and they feel proud of it."

But Richards said they may also feel more hesitant. "Older women have always been more likely to talk about abortion because for them it was something heroic," she said. "Younger women, we don't have to talk about it. That doesn't mean we're ashamed, but it's the same way I don't talk about having warts removed." Richards, thirty-four, recalled a conversation with some of her younger colleagues, who argued that the term "reproductive rights" should be replaced by "reproductive health and justice." "The younger women were saying 'reproductive rights' is a dated term," said Richards. "And they were right. I was too entrenched in my own view."

Women who consider abortion normal—such a given that it doesn't even count as a "right" but simply as "health and justice"—may also have more psychological space, not taken up by fears of injustice—to consider their own emotional, spiritual, or moral ambivalence about abortion.

But this lack of fear, the lack of historical perspective on the threats they may face in their lifetimes, the assumption that the right to control their bodies will never be snatched from them, are precisely why people like Susan Hill are so worried.

Hill is the president of the National Women's Health Organization, which runs women's health clinics in six midsize cities, including the only abortion clinic in Mississippi. "I have been so frustrated by hearing all this," said Hill, a trained social worker who has provided abortion services since the week after *Roe* was decided in 1973. "I am so frustrated by the apologetic approach toward abortion rights. It's so frustrating to hear people discussing the fetus but not discussing the woman.

"When I first started in the '70s, the image we saw was of a dead woman on the floor after an illegal abortion, with blood all around her. We were fighting for whether or not there were going to be dead women on dirty bathroom floors. We're two generations past that now, and that picture—well, you almost have to explain it to people who are in their twenties now, because, thank God, they've never had to see it."

She continued: "When I heard Hillary and Kerry saying we need more money for education, I thought, *This is crap! These are not uneducated women!*" Hill also dismissed as naive and classist the assumption that women born into a world where abortion is legal will never see their rights reversed. "This isn't going to end until the middle class and upper-middle class think it's going to affect them. Someone will always say, 'Rich women will always be able to get abortions.' But in cities where we're located, private doctors aren't doing private abortions. And this is when abortion is legal. I truly believe that if something changes with *Roe,* the wealthy and middle class will not be able to get [abortions] either. It's going to affect everybody."

She pointed out that despite improved sex-education programs and abstinence movements, the abortion rate has remained steady at between 1.3 million and 1.5 million abortions each year. "When I hear it should be 'safe but rare,' it makes me crazy," Hill said. "What's rare? What does that mean if it's been steady for thirty years that 1.3 million women needed abortions? I think it's a cop-out."

Hill also attacked the anti-abortion movement's focus on late-term abortions, pointing out that when she began providing services, there were very few second-trimester abortions. That changed in 1977, when the Hyde Amendment restricted Medicaid-funded abortions to poor women, who were then forced to save money and schedule later terminations. "The same people create a need for later abortions, and then they attack it! I think our community has lost sight of who we are fighting for. We have got to redefine it and give it a face again."

In this regard, Hill agrees with even the speakers who are driving her nuts. The movement needs energy, she said. "You have to make it personal to people."

Hill said that when she was in her twenties, an older doctor told her, "Before you start this, you have to sit down and search your soul. In the issue of abortion you have to identify with either the fetus or the woman, because at some point there's a choice and you cannot identify with both. You decide which one you're going to be the advocate for." Hill said firmly, "Thirty-two years later, my choice is always to help the woman."

There is, of course, no right answer, no correct choice. The notion that this many-years-later society is still working from the same two-pronged woman-or-fetus blueprint might be problematic. That blueprint could be exactly what's creating this internal pressure to evaluate, grow, and reach out before things get ugly again.

Almost exactly a year after the publication of Kissling's essay "Is There Life After *Roe?*" conservative judge Samuel Alito was confirmed to the Supreme Court, following the September 2005 confirmation of John Roberts. Just about a month after the addition of these two new justices to the bench, South Dakota passed a statewide ban on abortion, with almost no exceptions for rape or incest. It will likely find its way to the Supreme Court in the coming years as the next and terrifyingly, perhaps final, test of *Roe*. The fight has gotten scrappier, and will only get ugly in coming months and years. And the louder the discussions within the reproductive rights movement become, the further they demonstrate that Smeal was right to take the press to task for painting this moment as riven by internecine discord. In fact, what all the ideological jousting might suggest is not a movement coming apart at the seams but a community benefiting from the engaged, fresh, multigenerational vigor of internal debate that could—and in fact must—propel it into a new era. For the first time in decades, there seems to be a lot of life in the pro-choice movement.

AFTERWORD

GLORIA FELDT

Abortion isn't about abortion.

Perhaps it seems odd to say so in the afterword of a book in which women have looked prismatically at abortion. Yet I'm telling you—just after you've read this marvelous book, full of diverse and thought-provoking essays about abortion written by some remarkable women—that the issue of abortion is about so much more than abortion.

Just as René Magritte's painting, playfully named "This Is Not a Pipe," is a canvas covered with the image of a large pipe, abortion itself is not the thing that sticks in the craw of its zealous opponents. Abortion is a symbolic representation, merely a stand-in for the real thing. Considering this idea can have powerful meaning, which can instruct us when we put down this book and begin the strategic and political application of what we've learned from its pages. Perhaps our biggest challenge is to see the reality behind our own picture first.

It's important to define clearly what *we are* talking about and what *we want to be* talking about, because the perspective from which you start determines where you will end up in any conversation that has social and political ramifications. Whoever defines the debate topic usually wins it. Right now, all indicators—from the essays you just read to the daily news reports—seem to be telling us that we are on a path likely to end in a very bad place for women if we don't take charge of our own agenda without delay.

Here's what I think abortion is about, and what I believe we must do, not just to protect what's left of our human and civil rights to make our own childbearing decisions but to advance the cause of reproductive rights, healthcare access, and justice for all, for all time:

First, abortion is merely the tip of a huge ideological iceberg for both pro- and antichoice movements. It's code for a bigger agenda than we ever talk about in polite company.

We agonize over the surface story: South Dakota's new law to ban all abortions except those absolutely necessary to save a woman's life, with many other states copycatting; the litany of anti-abortion laws being passed at all levels of government, from the federal abortion ban to increasingly draconian restrictions on minors' access, to funding bans and gag rules, to mandatory delays and biased counseling that tries to dissuade women from choosing abortion, to attempts to make the FDA rescind its approval of mifepristone, to policies that allow healthcare providers to refuse to provide any service they wish. Abortion. Abortion. Abortion. Until people are sick and tired of fighting about it. Which is part of the anti-choice movement's strategy to wear us down.

But dive under the surface of this ocean and you begin to see that the anti-choice agenda is much larger than the issue of abortion. Just as politicians who vote against a woman's right to choose are far less likely than pro-choice officials to vote for funding for family-planning programs that prevent abortion or even for measures that help families provide for the support of children once they are born,[1] individuals and organizations that oppose abortion aren't necessarily, or even generally, in favor of contraception or concerned about the well-being of children once they are born.

I never call these people "pro-life," because they aren't. We who are pro-choice are far more pro-life in the final analysis. I, for one, know that the birth-control pill saved my life when I was a twenty-year-old wife and mother of three. It enabled me to be a better mother to my children. I do not consider the tubal sterilization I chose to have when I was thirty-two—so I wouldn't have to face another unintended pregnancy—a more life-affirming decision than another woman's decision to retain her fertility, knowing she would choose abortion if she became pregnant and did not want to be. After all, I met the love of my life a few years after my procedure and wanted to have a child with him. So there is one less "life" in this world today because I foreclosed the option of abortion for myself.

It makes no sense that those opposed to abortion are also more likely to oppose birth-control access or contraceptive coverage by insurance plans—that is, unless you understand what motivates their opposition. Fortunately, this is easier to see today than it was a few years ago. The election and then re-election of George W. Bush and an anti-choice Congress on the wings of the hard Right's takeover of the Republican Party, precinct by precinct during the last forty years, has emboldened them to climb out from under their anti-birth-control ice floes and hoist their true selves into the sunlight.

In addition to the fact that abortion is just the tip of the ideological iceberg, it is also my observation that these opposing ideologies reflect diametrically opposed worldviews about the nature and purpose of human sexuality. Worldviews stem from our most primal fears and wants.

So, like a best-selling novel, the debate over abortion comes down to struggles over sex and power, or more plainly, the power balance between men and women.

Recently, I appeared on Bill O'Reilly's *The O'Reilly Factor* opposite Wendy Wright, who represents the staunchly anti-choice Concerned Women for America. We were debating the appropriateness of a television ad for birth control. Wendy's taut face conveyed utter disgust as she sputtered on about how advertising contraception encouraged "recreational sex." I found myself wondering if she had ever experienced good recreational sex, or if perhaps she had experienced too much of it and was doing penance. Even Bill O'Reilly challenged her on the point that presumably providing birth control is the lesser evil if the choices were to come down to abortion or a couple having safe recreational sex. She emphatically disagreed. In fact, she seemed disgusted at the thought of sex for purposes other than procreation.

For the life of me, I could not fathom the Right's fixation on other people's sex lives until I came to realize what they are actually fixated on is fear that their world will be turned upside down when women have an equal place at life's table. They are, of course, correct that that's what would happen. Women *are* changing the status quo and the power balance between the genders—and we believe it's for the better. Technologies and policies that allow women to separate sex from childbearing represent positive steps toward justice. But these same advances represent a loss of power for those who have a stake in maintaining hierarchical control of the institutions of society.

Compare the rhetoric against birth control in 1916 (when the first birth-control clinic opened) to the rhetoric against abortion today, and you will see what I mean. Women, they warned, will become wanton hussies. The family will be weakened, children devalued. Our civilization will be corrupted. These same ideas, and even some of the same words, have been used throughout this 100-year battle. Explaining the American Life League's opposition to both abortion and birth control, its president, Judy Brown, said recently: "The mindset that invites a couple to use contraception is an antichild mindset."[2]

Most pro-choice people would argue precisely to the contrary; that it is life-enhancing to choose consciously to bear a child when one can properly nurture him or her. For me personally, reproductive freedom and justice, including abortion rights, became a lifelong passion because of my experiences as a mother, not because of an experience with abortion. Professionally, I speak as one who wore Margaret Sanger's mantle. And it fit all too well throughout my thirty years in the struggle for women's human right to make their own childbearing decisions because, though so much has changed, the underlying issues remain the same.

We are in a pitched battle to determine which of those worldviews will prevail. Yet it is a battleground not of our choosing, for while those of us on the pro-choice side are able to respect the views of those who oppose abortion, they are often unable to return that respect to us because their worldview brooks no such diversity. Often, they justify this rigid position with religious dogma.

After I appeared on *The O'Reilly Factor*, I received an email from someone who assured me that he was praying for my soul: "If you truly turned your life over to Christ, accepted Him as your Savior and Guide, and repented of your sins, you would have a new beginning. You would have a new understanding of what is right and what is wrong. You would believe just the opposite of what you believe now." Apparently, it never occurred to him that I arrived at my moral points of view about all this through my own faith and that I might interpret his message as a sin against women!

I opened this afterword by saying that abortion isn't about abortion. To make this point clear, organized opposition to abortion is either a cynical political calculation or smart politics, depending on your perspective, or perhaps your stake in the game. They lost the battle to keep women confined by their biology when birth control was legalized and embraced by 90 percent of society. The legalization of abortion provided just the flash point needed to energize true anti-choice believers and pull just enough of the morally unsure middle to their side. This keeps the political pot churning so that the issues never seem to get resolved. They want to make the debate be only about abortion in order to create a polarized focus on the fetus rather than the moral autonomy of women.

The Center for Reproductive Rights' well-documented study "If *Roe* Is Overturned" predicts that if we lose *Roe*—a scenario that seems more and more possible—thirty states will immediately move to outlaw abortion, as South Dakota has already done. This will most likely come true if we keep fighting about abortion and fail to insist upon broadening the debate. We need to insist that the debate address the issues of sex and power and whether women will ever secure simple justice. We should be able to stop pointing the finger of blame at ourselves for being in this pickle and keep it pointed toward the real culprits. Instead of being defensive, we can take charge, like Cecilia Fire Thunder, chief of the Oglala Sioux tribe in South Dakota, who pledged to start a reproductive health clinic on her reservation after the abortion ban was passed. "Americans," she said, "should be outraged about the number of women who are raped in this country. We need to also speak out for women in places like Afghanistan and other war-torn areas where rape is happening . . . Unfortunately, the world is not always a safe place for women. Ultimately, this is a much bigger issue than just abortion. The women of America should be outraged that policies and decisions about their bodies are being made by male politicians and clergy. It's time for women to reclaim their bodies."[3] Yes, indeed, it is time; and leave it to a woman named Fire Thunder to say so with clarity.

So, then, where do we go from here?

We must first build a durable human rights basis for reproductive justice that includes as a matter of course the legal rights, moral framework, and practical access to birth control, accurate and comprehensive sex education, and economic justice that allow women to make uncoerced childbearing decisions, whether begetting, bearing, or choosing not to bear.

The right to make our own decisions about sex and childbearing is the most fundamental human and civil right. We own that moral high ground. We simply have to name it, claim it, and stand steadfastly upon it. This is the framework from which we must speak at all times, despite the challenges of doing so. This is also the framework from which we must shape and advance an aggressive agenda.

The writer Sally Kempton has said, "It's hard to fight an enemy who has outposts in your head." We must clear our heads so that we can set the agenda where we want it to be in regard to reproductive rights, as well as universal access to the healthcare and information services that give rights meaning. We can fight on our terms and our turf and make those who oppose women's most fundamental human and civil rights fight on the battlefield of our choosing.

But this is not just about message; it is essential to advance a strong positive and proactive agenda. I think it is important both strategically and for the soul of a movement to keep moving forward.

The time is ripe to mount a stirring campaign to pass the Prevention First Act (PFA) in Congress and in the states. The PFA would significantly increase access to family-planning services, require that sex education be medically accurate (abstinence-only won't do), expand public knowledge about and access to emergency contraception, and more. Placing the focus on prevention is wise politically because it can bring the largest coalition to the table, since 90 percent of Americans support access to birth control. They know that's what prevents the need for abortion. Most important to me, access to contraceptive services gives women the basic healthcare they need to be healthy and responsible about their own lives.

Inevitably, by raising the issue of increasing access to contraception, we also begin to smoke out the real anti-choice agenda and make it transparent to all. We can then engage the morally unsure middle in these positive efforts and bring ever more of them into our efforts.

But we can't stop with prevention bills, as important as they are. We must ultimately address head-on the underlying human rights question of who has moral and legal autonomy over begetting and/or bearing children. To do that, we must build from the grassroots up to pass Freedom of Choice Acts at the state and federal levels. This legislation will have the effect of codifying the principle that no one can be discriminated against if they choose to have or not to have a child. It's simple justice for women.

No question about it, this is a tall order that will likely take another generation to achieve. But we must learn from our own history so that we can repeat it. And we must tell our own stories so that dry words like "rights" and "access" will touch hearts as well as minds.

The ascendancy of birth control as a health service and a social movement succeeded in the twentieth century because it gave society a positive vision. It met people's real needs in tangible, personal ways. To fend off current assaults on all our reproductive rights, including abortion, the pro-choice movement absolutely must put forth a clear and positive twenty-first century vision, one that resonates for people today. Merely responding to attacks or even fighting back won't do; in fact, it will make things worse. We must come roaring forward with a strong message, a compelling policy agenda, and a bold initiative to expand reproductive health services.

The essays in this book contain many juicy, thought-provoking perspectives to help us along the way. And I believe we are in a moment of opportunity unlike any we have experienced for decades, a moment in which the time is ripe to advance both the messages and the policies that will allow women's reproductive self-determination to flourish. This can and will happen if we join together, embracing our diversity of perspectives, and commit to bringing true reproductive justice home for the next generation of women.

Motherhood in freedom is a human rights ideal that is steeped in our highest values as a society. We own that ground. Let us cultivate it well.

Gloria Feldt *is a women's health and rights advocate from the point where the personal and the political meet. The author of* The War on Choice: The Right-Wing Attack on Women's Rights and How to Fight Back *(Bantam, 2004) and* Behind Every Choice Is a Story *(University of North Texas Press, 2003), she is currently writing a book with the actress Kathleen Turner on Turner's life lessons for women. Ms. Feldt led Planned Parenthood affiliates in West Texas and Arizona for twenty-two years, and she served as national president of Planned Parenthood Federation of America from 1996–2005. She now speaks nationally in an independent voice about women, health, leadership, and politics. As a teen mother who became the leader of the nation's largest reproductive health and advocacy organization, she has been dubbed "the voice of experience" by* People *magazine.*

ACKNOWLEDGMENTS

Writing is usually solitary work, but putting an anthology together is deeply collaborative. I could not have brought this project to fruition without the generous help and support of both friends and new acquaintances.

I owe a world of gratitude to my editor, Brooke Warner, for helping to create the vision for this book. Brooke is articulate, smart, and well-read on political matters; she is also, to my benefit, a pragmatic visionary with tremendous editorial skill. I am indebted to her for the support and kindness she has shown me.

Special thanks to: Margaret (Peg) Johnston, Karen Kubby, Pat Sandin, Rebecca Walker, Gloria Feldt, Chrisse France, Terry Reed, Grayson Dempsey, Claire Keyes, Victoria Tepe, Hanne Blank, Amy Richards, Charlotte Taft, Jennifer Baumgardner, Amy Hagstrom Miller, and Kudra MacCaillech, whose words and actions inspire and illuminate me.

Thanks are also due to my good friends: Emari Dimagiba, Ahndi Fridell, Melisse Gelula, Mary Pat Rice, Ashley Sovereign, Elizabeth Wardle, and Lauri Wollner, for the strength and courage they give me, and for their support along the arduous path to publication.

I am grateful to Rhonda Chittenden, a friend and colleague in reproductive health education, for spending her precious lunch hours listening to my ideas and sharing thoughtful advice.

My gratitude also goes to my husband Jim, who always encourages and supports me, and to my sons, Maxwell and Colin. My life is blessed because our paths are joined.

And finally, my deepest thanks to the contributors of this book for adding to my own insight and wisdom about abortion.

RESOURCES: EDITOR'S NOTE

There are hundreds of thousands of websites about abortion. Some are good, many are not. The most harmful sites are the ones that purport to be unbiased and nonjudgmental but possess varying degrees of anti-abortion messages embedded in them. These messages attempt to steer women into choosing parenthood or adoption and they usually have inaccurate and judgment-laden information about abortion. These sites are carefully crafted to manipulate people who are in crisis and who desperately need nonjudgmental and accurate information about their options.

One of the best and most comprehensive sites available today is ChoiceLinkUp.Com: The Pro-Choice Web Ring (www.choicelinkup .com). This site contains a comprehensive directory of sites that have accurate information about reproductive rights and health, as well as a list of pro-choice organizations and discussion sites.

This site is trustworthy and is well-researched. I highly recommend it to anyone in search of resources about reproductive health and pregnancy options.

NOTES

Sex, Unintended Pregnancy, and Poverty

1. In their groundbreaking volume *Conceiving the New World Order* (University of California Press, 1995), Faye Ginsburg and Rayna Rapp introduced the notion of "stratified reproduction," or "the power relations by which some categories of people are empowered to nurture and reproduce, while others are disempowered." This model highlights how reproductive practices—and, I would add, care and treatment—vary greatly along lines of class, race, and other axes of inequality. Ginsburg and Rapp say that a woman's ability to protect herself and/or her partner(s) from unwanted pregnancy and disease depends greatly on social power and privilege.

2. Silliman, J. M., M. G. Fried, L. Ross, and E. R. Gutierrez. *Undivided Rights: Women of Color Organize for Reproductive Justice.* Cambridge: South End Press, 2004.

3. Petchesky, R. P. and K. Judd, eds. *Negotiating Reproductive Rights: Women's Perspectives Across Countries and Cultures.* New York: Zed Books, 1998.

4. Higgins, J. "The Pleasure Deficit: The Role of Desire in Contraceptive Use." PhD dissertation. Atlanta: Emory University, 2005.

A New Vision For Advancing our Movement for Reproductive Health, Reproductive Rights, and Reproductive Justice

1. Ross, L. "Revisions to the ACRJ Reproductive Justice Paper." Email to the author. August 3, 2005.

2. Planned Parenthood Federation of America. "*Roe v. Wade:* Its History and Impact." October 3, 2005. www.plannedparenthood.org.

3. Miller B. A., L. N. Kolonel, L. Bernstein, J.L. Young, Jr., G. M. Swanson, D. West, C. R. Key, J. M. Liff, C. S. Glover, G. A. Alexander, et al., eds. *Racial/Ethnic Patterns of Cancer in the United States 1988-1992.* National Institutes of Health Pub. No. 96-4104. Bethesda, MD: National Cancer Institute, 1996.

4. Roberts, D. "Race, Reproduction, and the Meaning of Liberty: Building A Social Justice Vision of Reproductive Freedom." April 18, 2000. Public forum presented by The Othmer Institute at Planned Parenthood New York City.

5. Berer, M. "Sexuality, Rights and Social Justice." *Reproductive Health Matters* 12.23 (2004): 6-11.

6. Ibid.

7. Ibid.

8. Ibid.

9. Ross, op. cit.

10. Burlingame, P. "Sex Education in California Public Schools." Released August 2003 by ACLU of Northern California.

11. Environmental Working Group. "Skin Deep Executive Summary." June 2004. www.ewg.org/reports/skindeep/report/executive_summary.php.

We Have Met the Enemy, and She/He Is Us

1. Kelly, W. "Zeroing In on Those Polluters: We Have Met the Enemy and He Is Us." *The Best of Pogo.* Ed. W. Kelly and B. Crouch, Jr. New York: Simon & Schuster, 1982.

2. Birmingham, Alabama was the site of a 1998 bombing by Eric Rudolph that killed a security guard and maimed a nurse.

3. Major, B. and R. Gramzow. "Abortion as Stigma: Cognitive and Emotional Implications of Concealment." *Journal of Personality and Social Psychology* 77 (1999): 735-46.

4. I explored this theme thoroughly in "From the Birmingham Bombing to September 11: Opting Out of the Abortion War," in *Our Choices, Our Lives: Unapologetic Writings on Abortion.* Ed. K. Jacob. Lincoln, Nebraska: iUniverse, 2004.

5. Major, B., op. cit. In this study, fewer than 25 percent of women told

their parents, but this may have changed now that parental-notification laws are in effect in thirty-four states.

6. For this and other conversation-starters, go to www.abortion conversation.com.

7. The Abortion Conversation Project and Exhale. "Report from an Exploratory Meeting on Post-Abortion Emotional Health." November 2000. www.abortionconversation.com.

8. Major, B., C. Cozzarelli, M. L. Cooper, J. Zubek, C. Richards, M. Wilhite, and R. Gramzow. "Psychological Responses of Women Following First Trimester Abortion." *Archives of General Psychiatry* 57 (2000): 777-84.

9. National Coalition of Abortion Providers. "Post-Abortion Emotional Health." December 20, 2002.

10. www.momimpregnant.com, www.dadimpregnant.com, websites of the Abortion Conversation Project.

11. Only seventeen states use their own funds to pay for Medicaid-eligible women's medically necessary abortions. www.aclu.org.

12. The National Network of Abortion Funds. www.nnaf.org.

13. Tolman, D. *Dilemmas of Desire: Teenage Girls Talk about Sexuality.* Cambridge: Harvard University Press, 2002.

The Rhetoric of Abortion:
Reflections from a Former Pro-Life Activist

1. Stassen, G. "Pro-Life? Look at the Fruits." *Sojourners* October 13, 2004. www.sojo.net/.

2. Ibid.

3. Stassen, G. "New Data Informs Abortion Rate Debate." *Sojourners* June 2, 2005. www.sojo.net/.

Unspoken Loss: The Experience of "Therapeutic" and Late-Term Abortion

1. Voss, Gretchen. "My Late-Term Abortion." *The Boston Globe* January 25, 2004.

2. Ginty, Molly M. "Late-Term Abortion Saved These Women's Lives." *Women's eNews* October, 28, 2004.

3. Weil, Elizabeth. "A Wrongful Birth?" *The New York Times Magazine* March 12, 2006.

Abortion by Any Other Name

1. Haskell, M. "Dilation and Extraction for Late Second Trimester Abortion." Presented at the National Abortion Federation Risk Management Seminar. Dallas, TX. September 13, 1992.

2. Centers for Disease Control and Prevention. "Abortion Surveillance-United States, 2000." *Morbidity and Mortality Weekly Report* 52.SS12 (2003): 1-32.

3. Ibid.

The Politics of Fetal Pain

1. Lee, S. J, H. J. Ralston, E. A. Drey, J. C. Partridge, and M. A. Rosen. "Fetal Pain: A Systematic, Multidisciplinary Review of the Evidence." *Journal of the American Medical Association* 294.8 (2005): 947-54.

2. Donovan, P. "Judging Teenagers: How Minors Fare When They Seek Court-authorized Abortions." *Family Planning Perspectives* 15.16 (1983): 259-67.

3. Ellertson, C. "Mandatory Parental Involvement in Minors' Abortions: Effects of the Laws in Minnesota, Missouri, and Indiana." *American Journal of Public Health* 87.8 (1997): 1367-74.

4. Joyce T. and R. Kaestner. "State Reproductive Policies and Adolescent Pregnancy Resolution: The Case of Parental Involvement Laws." *Journal of Health Economics* 15 (1996): 579-607.

5. Appelbaum, P. S. and T. Grisso. "Assessing Patients' Capacities to Consent to Treatment." *New England Journal of Medicine* 319.25 (1998): 1635-8.

Roth, L., A. Meisel, and C. Lidz. "Tests of Competency to Consent to Treatment." *American Journal of Psychiatry* 134 (1977): 279-84.

Tepper, A. M. and A. Elwork. "Competence to Consent to Treatment as a Psycholegal Construct." *Law and Human Behavior* 8.3/4 (1984): 205-23.

Welie, J.V.M. and S. P. K. Welie. "Patient Decision-Making Competence: Outlines of a Conceptual Analysis." *Medicine, Health Care and Philosophy* 4 (2001): 127-38.

I'm Not Sorry

1. Henshaw, Stanley K. "Unintended Pregnancy in the United States." *Family Planning Perspectives* January/February 1998: 24-9, 46.

2. The number of providers in 2000 was 37 percent lower than the all-time high of 2,908 in 1982. Finer, Lawrence B. and Stanley K. Henshaw. "The Accessibility of Abortion Services in the United States, 2001." *Perspectives on Sexual and Reproductive Health* 35.1 (2003): 16-24.

3. South Carolina, which has had a state version of the Unborn Victims of Violence Act since 1984, has convicted only one man of murder based on fetal personhood. By contrast, fifty to 100 pregnant women have been arrested due to claims of fetal personhood.

4. Children's Defense Fund. "13 Million Children Face Food Insecurity." June 2, 2004. http://childrensdefense.org/.

5. This would more accurately be called a "chromosomal sex test," since it would not identify tomboys or flaming boys other than differentiating their biological sexes.

6. McCurry, Justin and Rebecca Allison. " 'One Child' Policy Leaves China with Huge Shortage of Women." *The Guardian*, London. March 23, 2004. Among demographers working on this issue, estimates of

missing women and girls vary considerably above and below forty million, depending on the methods used and the age groups examined.

7. Picard, Andre. "Sex-Selection Tests in India Mean Fewer Girls, Study Says." *Globe and Mail*, Toronto. January 9, 2005.

8. Landsburg, Steven. "Oh, No: It's a Girl! Do Daughters Cause Divorce?" *Slate*. October 2, 2003. www.slate.com/id/2089142.

"I Had an Abortion" and Other Ululations

1. McFalls, Jr., J. A. "Population: A Lively Introduction." *Population Bulletin* December 2003.

2. The Guttmacher Institute. "An Overview of Abortion in the United States."http://agi-usa.org/media/presskits/2005/06/28/abortionover view.html.

3. Feldt, G. *The War on Choice: The Right-Wing Attack on Women's Rights and How to Fight Back*. New York: Bantam Books, 2004. 11.

4. Mosher, W. D., et al. "Use Of Contraception and Use of Family Planning Services in the United States: 1982-2002." *Advance Data from Vital and Health Statistics* 350 (2004): 2. Ninety percent of women ages fifteen to forty-four who have ever had intercourse have used a condom, and 82 percent have used the Pill.

5. Solinger, R. *Abortion Wars: A Half-Century of Struggle, 1950-2000*. Berkeley and Los Angeles: University of California Press, 1998. 4.

Twice Is a Spanking

1. According to Planned Parenthood, two out of every 100 women aged fifteen to forty-four will have an abortion this year and half of them have had at least one abortion previously.

Afterword

1. Schroedel, J. R. *Is the Fetus a Person?: A Comparison of Policies Across the Fifty States*. Ithaca: Cornell University Press, 2000.

2. Shorto, Russell. "The War on Contraception." *The New York Times Magazine* May 7, 2006.

3. Agular, Rose. "The Power of Thunder." *AlterNet* April 4, 2006. www .alternet.org.

ABOUT THE CONTRIBUTORS

Jennifer Baumgardner, a writer and activist, is the coauthor of *Manifesta: Young Women, Feminism, and the Future* (Farrar, Straus and Giroux, 2000) and *Grassroots: A Field Guide for Feminist Activism* (Farrar, Straus and Giroux, 2005) and the author of *Look Both Ways* (Farrar, Straus and Giroux, 2007), a book about bisexuality and feminism. She is the creator of the "I Had an Abortion" campaign, which aims to destigmatize abortion. Originally from Fargo, North Dakota, she lives in New York with her toddler, Skuli.

Alana Bibeau is a teacher, poet, wannabe midwife, and doctoral candidate in sociology at a conservative Southern university. She lives in a crooked old house with slanted ceilings and wide-slat wooden floorboards with her two dogs. In between teaching, writing, and activism, she spends her time holding tea parties with dead poets and wishing on the moon.

Founded in 1989, **Asian Communities for Reproductive Justice (ACRJ)** has been at the forefront of building a Reproductive Justice Movement that places the reproductive health and rights of Asian women and girls within a social justice framework. ACRJ uses core strategies of community organizing and movement building to work toward the liberation of Asian women and girls through the lens of reproductive justice.

Bon and **Lou** are the fictitious names of two pregnancy counselors with dozens of years of experience working in abortion clinics. All of the names and many of the details in their blog entries have been changed. More stories can be accessed at www.abortionclinicdays.com.

Laura Fraser is freelance writer who has written about women's health issues for two decades. She is the author of *Losing It: America's Obsession with Weight and the Industry that Feeds On It* (Dutton, 1997); *An*

Italian Affair (Vintage, 2002); and co-wrote *The War on Choice* (Bantam, 2004) with Gloria Feldt, past president of the Planned Parenthood Federation of America. Ms. Fraser has written for many national magazines, including *O, Vogue, Glamour, Self, Marie Claire, Mother Jones, Vogue, More, Mode, Gourmet, Food & Wine, Bon Appetit, Salon.com, The San Francisco Examiner Magazine, The New York Times Magazine, Mirabella, Health, Good Housekeeping, Ladies' Home Journal,* and *The Progressive.*

Jenny Higgins is a postdoctoral fellow in HIV, sexuality, and gender at Columbia University. Her primary research interest is the influence of sexual pleasure on contraceptive and condom use in the United States and abroad. She has conducted research on reproductive health and abortion at organizations such as the Guttmacher Institute, Ipas, the Empowerment of Women Research Program, and the Centers for Disease Control and Prevention. As an abortion activist, she conducts one phone shift a week with WRRAP (the Women's Reproductive Rights Action Project, www.wrrap.org), a national abortion fund (www.nnaf .org). Since her recent move to Manhattan, she has also volunteered with the Haven Coalition, an underground network of women who provide housing for women seeking abortions in New York City. When she's not out being a feminist, she's either swimming, running, or hanging out with her family on Peaks Island, Maine.

Diana Huet de Guerville currently works as a grassroots organizer for Planned Parenthood League of Massachusetts in Springfield, Massachusetts. She has a master's degree in environmental studies from York University focused on feminist resistance to globalization, and has published several articles related to women's rights and social justice. An activist for many years, Huet de Guerville has also worked as a union organizer and environmental educator, among many other adventures in the wacky world of progressive politics.

Margaret R. Johnston has been the director of Southern Tier Women's Services in upstate New York since 1981, and has served as president of both the Abortion Conversation Project and the National Coalition of Abortion Providers. She is the creator of the *Pregnancy Options Workbook* and *ChoiceLinkup.com*. She is a leader in developing messaging directly from the abortion experience and has developed counseling-training aids and patient education.

Writer, advocate, and policy analyst **Frances Kissling** is president of Catholics for a Free Choice (CFFC), an international, non-governmental organization that advances reproductive health, women's rights, and the strengthening of civil society through research, education, and policy analysis. CFFC is a leading force for change in the Catholic Church. Ms. Kissling has been called "the philosopher of the pro-choice movement," and is widely regarded as one of the most thoughtful and eloquent voices on a range of critical issues in religion, reproductive health, and women's rights. Ms. Kissling puts forward a moral perspective on the right to choose abortion that includes a passionate commitment to the moral agency of women and a deep respect for life. Kissling has briefed parliamentarians and development professionals on reproductive health and rights, religion and public policy in a number of countries including Brazil, Mexico, the Philippines, Germany, Ireland, the United Kingdom, Poland, and the United States. Kissling's essay has been excerpted from an original article that appeared in *Conscience: The Newsjournal of Catholic Opinion* published quarterly by Catholics for a Free Choice. The full version is available at www.catholicsforchoice.org /conscience/archives/c2004win_lifeafterroe.asp.

Jacqueline Lalley is a writer, poet, and communications consultant for nonprofits. Her work has appeared in *The Onion, Bitch, The Harvard Review*, and other publications. Her essay "Evidence" was published in *Secrets & Confidences: The Complicated Truth about Women's Friendships* (Seal Press, 2004).

Raised in Anchorage, Alaska by first-generation immigrants, **Pandora L. Leong** has volunteered for issues ranging from aid to low-income women to advocacy for queer youth and communities of color, in addition to domestic violence and reproductive justice, for over ten years. Her publications include "Living Outside the Box" in *Colonize This! Young Women of Color on Today's Feminism* (Seal Press, 2002). Leong aspires to help create a feminist world, free of violence and misogyny and the tyranny of chocolate on dessert menus.

Alissa Perrucci writes and consults in the area of abortion access and abortion counseling. For three years, she worked as an abortion and pregnancy options counselor in Pittsburgh, Pennsylvania. She has a PhD in psychology from Duquesne University and an MPH from the University of California, Berkeley.

Amy Richards is presently at work on *Opting In: The Case for Motherhood and Feminism* (forthcoming by Farrar, Straus and Giroux). She is also the coauthor of *Manifesta: Young Women, Feminism, and the Future* (Farrar, Straus and Giroux, 2000) and *Grassroots: A Field Guide to Feminist Activism* (Farrar, Straus and Giroux, 2005).

Carolina De Robertis is a cofounder of Exhale, the nation's first after-abortion talkline that respects reproductive freedom. As Exhale's first program director, she oversaw the talkline's growth into a multilingual, national service, and conducted workshops on transforming abortion stigma for providers throughout the Americas. She is currently completing her first novel, which chronicles four generations of Uruguayan women. She lives with her wife in Oakland, California.

Victoria Tepe holds a PhD in psychology and behavioral neuroscience from Northwestern University. Her professional history includes research, teaching, writing, and publication in the areas of reproductive rights and domestic violence. She also serves on the board of the national Abortion Conversation Project and is a member of the Community Advisory Board for the Four Women Reproductive Health Center in Attleboro, Massachusetts.

Rebecca Traister is a staff writer at *Salon.com,* where she writes about women in politics, media, and entertainment. She lives in Brooklyn, New York.

Patricia Justine Tumang is an activist, writer, and member of the queer Pinay artists collective Kreatibo. Her writing, which reflects her commitment to social justice from a queer Filipina American perspective, has appeared in *Waking Up American: Growing Up Biculturally, Colonize This! Young Women of Color on Today's Feminism,* and *Hyphen Magazine.* She is the coeditor of the upcoming Seal Press anthology tentatively titled *Homelands: Women's Journeys Toward Meanings of Home* (2007). She received her MFA in English and creative writing from Mills College in Oakland, California, where she currently resides.

Elizabeth Wardle, PhD, teaches rhetoric and writing as an assistant professor in the English department at the University of Dayton in Dayton, Ohio. She and her husband of seven years have chosen not to have children. She pours most of her energy into researching issues related to the teaching and learning of writing. She is currently working on a book about public misconceptions of writing.

Lauri Wollner was born and raised in Iowa. She has a bachelor's degree in psychology and a master's degree in rehabilitation counseling.

She has worked with persons with disabilities, as a chemical dependency counselor, and as a counselor for a GLBT substance abuse treatment center. Since 1998, she has been employed with a leading AIDS service organization that provides HIV-prevention information and referral services for persons living with HIV/AIDS. Being a butch, queer woman, Wollner endures the uglier side of humanity but still stands tall and lives with integrity. She credits her spirituality as her main survival tool. She enjoys camping with her friends and close family members. She currently lives with her partner of nearly ten years, three cats, and a snake named Miss Celie.

ABOUT THE EDITOR

Krista Jacob has a master's degree in women's studies from Minnesota State University, Mankato. She worked as an advocate and counselor for victims of rape and domestic violence for over a decade. At the Midwest Health Center for Women, she provided abortion counseling for women and girls, as well as indecision counseling for women coping with unplanned pregnancies. She is the editor of *Our Choices, Our Lives: Unapologetic Writings on Abortion* (iUniverse Star, 2002). She is a full-time writer and mother of two young sons.

CREDITS

An earlier version of "Is There Life After *Roe?* How to Think about the Fetus," by Frances Kissling first appeared in the Winter 2004-2005 issue of *Conscience: The Newsjournal of Catholic Opinion,* published by Catholics for a Free Choice, www.conscience-magazine.org.

"What Is Abortion?" by Amy Richards first appeared in the Winter 2005-2005 issue of *Conscience: The Newsjournal of Catholic Opinion,* published by Catholics for a Free Choice, www.conscience-magazine.org.

An earlier version of "Mifepristone" by Laura Fraser originally appeared in *Self* magazine.

"*Nasaan ka anak ko?* A Queer Filipina American Feminist's Tale of Abortion and Self-Recovery" by Patricia Justine Tumang was first published in *Colonize This! Young Women of Color on Today's Feminism* (Seal Press, 2002).

An earlier version of "Twice Is a Spanking" by Jennifer Baumgardner was published on *Slate.*

"Morality Play" by Rebecca Traister first appeared on *Salon.* An online version remains in the Salon archives. Reprinted with permission.

SELECTED TITLES FROM SEAL PRESS

For more than thirty years, Seal Press has published groundbreaking books. By women. For women. Visit our website at www.sealpress.com.

Above Us Only Sky: A Woman Looks Back, Ahead, and into the Mirror by Marion Winik. $14.95. 1-58005-144-8. A witty and engaging book from NPR commentator Marion Winik about facing midlife without getting tangled up in the past or hung up in the future.

Cunt: A Declaration of Independence by Inga Muscio. $14.95, 1-58005-075-1. "An insightful, sisterly, and entertaining exploration of the word and the part of the body it so bluntly defines. Ms. Muscio muses, reminisces, pokes into history and emerges with suggestions for the understanding of—and reconciliation with—what it means to have a cunt." —Roberta Gregory, author of *Naughty Bitch*

The F-Word: Feminism in Jeopardy by Kristin Rowe-Finkbeiner. $14.95, 1-58005-114-6. An astonishing look at the tenuous state of women's rights and issues in America, and a call to action for the young women who have the power to change their situation.

Intimate Politics: How I Grew Up Red, Fought for Free Speech and Became a Feminist Rebel by Bettina F. Aptheker. $15.95, 1-58005-160-X. A courageous and uncompromising account of one woman's personal and political transformation during a key chapter in our nation's history.

Pissed Off: On Women and Anger by Spike Gillespie. $14.95, 1-58005-162-6. An amped up and personal self-help book that encourages women to go ahead and use that middle finger without being closed off to the notion of forgiveness.

A Matter of Choice: 25 People Who Have Transformed Their Lives edited by Joan Chatfield-Taylor. $14.95, 1-58005-118-9. An inspiring collection of essays by people who made profound changes in their work, personal life, location, or lifestyle, proving that it is indeed never too late to take the road less traveled.